W9-BCA-824

Pillsbury™

fast & healthy
meals for kids

Houghton Mifflin Harcourt
Boston New York

General Mills

Editorial Director: Jeff Nowak

Publishing Manager: Christine Gray

Editor: Grace Wells

Recipe Development and Testing:
Pillsbury Kitchens

Photography: General Mills
Photography Studios and Image
Library

Photographer: Val Bourassa

Food Stylists: Barb Standal,
Susan Brosious

Publisher: Natalie Chapman

Associate Publisher: Jessica
Goodman

Executive Editor: Anne Ficklen

Editor: Adam Kowit

Editorial Assistant: Cecily McAndrews

Production Editor: Abby Saul

Cover Design: Suzanne Sunwoo

Art Director: Tai Blanche

Interior Design and Layout:
Holly Wittenberg

Manufacturing Manager: Kevin Watt

This book is printed on acid-free paper. ∞

Copyright © 2010 by General Mills, Minneapolis, Minnesota. All rights reserved.

Published by Houghton Mifflin Harcourt Publishing Company

Published simultaneously in Canada

For information about permission to reproduce selections from this book,
write to trade.permissions@hmhco.com or to Permissions,
Houghton Mifflin Harcourt Publishing Company,
3 Park Avenue, 19th Floor, New York, New York 10016.

www.hmhco.com

Library of Congress Cataloging-in-Publication Data
Pillsbury fast & healthy meals for kids.
   p. cm.
 Includes index.
 ISBN 978-0-470-64725-7 (cloth)
 1. Quick and easy cookery. 2. Children--Nutrition. I. Title: Fast & healthy meals for kids.
 TX833.5.P549 2010
 641.5'55—dc22
                              2010010593

Manufactured in China
TOP 10 9 8 7 6 5
4500747708

Cover photo: Blueberry-Pomegranate Smoothies (page 38), the Pizza Chicken and Ravioli (page 90), Easy Cocoa Brownies (page 176), and Whole-Grain Waffles (page 18).

Home of the Pillsbury Bake-Off® Contest

Pillsbury

Our recipes have been
tested in the Pillsbury Kitchens
and meet our standards of easy
preparation, reliability and great taste.

For more great recipes, visit **pillsbury.com**

dear families,

Fast, tasty and good for you too—what a winning concept! Plus, your kids will actually want to eat these recipes. The choices in this book were meant to appeal to kids, but we also wanted the rest of the family to like them too. And, understanding that food preferences can vary greatly (even for kids), you'll find a variety of flavors represented.

Also, throughout the book, there are tips to substitute ingredients and easy ideas for additions to meals so that you can customize as you and your family like.

All of the recipes follow guidelines from our nutrition experts at the Bell Institute of Nutrition so you can be sure that they are lower in fat and calories than most recipes. We recognize the importance of family meals and great food but also know that time is at a premium too, so all of the recipes are ready in 30 minutes or less.

Check out our practical guidelines up-front for helping kids to eat healthy and build an active lifestyle. We've included MyPyramid for kids from the USDA, an added bonus for showing kids how to make healthy food choices. Then, look for Doughboy Tips scattered throughout the book providing ideas for kids to help with food preparation—what fun they can have in the kitchen if they follow the Doughboy's Kitchen Clues for Kids on page 9.

Eating healthy meals as a family and creating good examples for kids is essential as they grow. With this book of kid-approved recipes and ideas, you're on the right track.

We're delighted to share this *Fast & Healthy Meals for Kids* cookbook with you. Enjoy!

Grace Wells
Editor

contents

healthy eating for kids
choosing healthy foods

Just for Kids! Did you know about the food guidance system called *MyPyramid for Kids?* It's a great resource that mom or dad can help kids check out. It shows colorful, fun graphics about how to make healthy choices for eating right, getting exercise and having fun.

MyPyramid for Kids can help youngsters learn how to include a variety of foods from each of the food groups every day. Follow the information below and have kids enjoy a rainbow of colors at every meal each day to meet their body's needs. Serving size and nutrition in this book are a general guideline. Kids may eat smaller servings.

healthy foods in right amounts

Now that we've provided some basics about the different foods to eat, let's look at how much children actually need according to *MyPyramid for Kids*. The **right amount** of food from each food group depends upon age, boy versus girl and the amount of physical activity a child gets. Here's a table showing the right amounts for kids ages 4–13 years. Children younger than age 4, teens older than age 13 and adults will have different needs.

how many servings is right for me?

GROUP	GIRLS & BOYS 4-8 years	GIRLS 9-13 years	BOYS 9-13 years
Grains	4-5-ounce equivalents*	5-ounce equivalents*	6-ounce equivalents*
Vegetables	1½ cups	2 cups	2½ cups
Fruits	1-1½ cups	1½ cups	1½ cups
Milk	2 cups	3 cups	3 cups
Meat & Beans	3-4-ounce equivalents**	5-ounce equivalents**	5-ounce equivalents**

*A 1-ounce equivalent of Grains: 1 slice of bread, 1 cup ready-to-eat cereal, ½ cup cooked rice, ½ cup cooked pasta, ½ cup cooked oatmeal, 1 small tortilla, 5 whole grain crackers or 3 cups popped popcorn.

**A 1-ounce equivalent of Meats & Beans: 1 ounce meat, poultry or fish, ¼ cup cooked dry beans, ¼ cup tofu, 1 egg, 1 tablespoon peanut butter, 2 tablespoons hummus, or ½ ounce nuts or seeds.

what's an ounce equivalent?

To compare foods by calories and the nutrients they provide, *MyPyramid for Kids* uses ounce equivalents for both the Grains group and the Meats & Beans group. In this way, a serving of foods within those food groups is similar to others from the same food group—but the right amount of the serving may be different from one ounce. Servings from the Fruit and Vegetable groups may vary too depending upon whether they're cooked or raw.

active family fun

Being healthy is also about the things kids do—not just what they eat. It's important to make healthy choices about how to live an active life. Here are some ideas for kids and their families to share, have some fun and keep moving!

- Have an activity party for a child's birthday. Backyard competitions, bowling, relay races, soccer, mini-golf, even interactive electronic fitness games (such as Wii) can keep kids on the move.

- Suggest setting up a family home gym that kids can help with. Use canned foods as weights, a rope for jumping and stairs for climbing. Don't forget that stretching is important too!

- Find time each day to be active. Kids can play catch, walk the dog and jump in the leaves. It all counts for daily exercise.

- Create a chart or calendar and keep track of family activities. Give everyone a different color or symbol and have a contest to see who logs the most activity.

6 healthy tips for kids to remember

Besides eating a variety of foods, it's important to follow some healthy principles daily. Here's what you want to do, kids:

1 Be **active** every day—at least 60 minutes daily.

2 **Choose** healthier foods from each food group. That means low-fat options that are full of vitamins and minerals to help you grow big and strong.

3 **Eat more** from some groups than others. Limit fats and sweets but enjoy other healthy choices.

4 Every **color** every day means eat a variety of foods—fruits, veggies, grains, dairy, meats!

5 Make choices that are **right for you**— not what's right for your friends.

6 Take **one step** at a time—that means make easy changes little by little.

MyPyramid For Kids
Eat Right. Exercise Have Fun.
MyPyramid.gov

Grains — Make half your grains whole
Vegetables — Vary your veggies
Fruits — Focus on fruits
Milk — Get your calcium-rich foods
Meat & Beans — Go lean with protein

Oils — Oils are not a food group, but you need some for good health. Get your oils from fish, nuts, and liquid oils such as corn oil, soybean oil, and canola oil.

Find your balance between food and fun   Fats and sugars — know your limits

FRUITS *(Apples, Bananas, Blueberries, Grapes, Oranges, Pears, Pineapple, Raisins, Strawberries)*

- Focus on eating nature's treats every day.
- Fruits are sweet and delicious and provide vitamins, minerals and fiber.
- Fruits help keep tissues healthy and provide kids with energy.

MILK *(Cheese, Milk, Yogurt)*

- Serve plenty of milk at every meal.
- Be sure milk or yogurt is low fat or fat free.
- Calcium-rich dairy foods help build strong bones and teeth.

GRAINS *(Breads, Cereal, Couscous, Oatmeal, Pasta, Rice, Tortillas)*

- Start smart with a breakfast of cereal made with whole grain.
- Make half of the grains every day whole.
- Grains provide carbohydrates for energy to keep kids running and playing hard.

VEGETABLES *(Asparagus, Carrots, Corn, Broccoli, Green Beans, Peas, Squash, Tomatoes)*

- Add color to meals with great-tasting veggies that are green and orange.
- Vegetables add vitamins, minerals and fiber to meals.
- They help kids to see and taste, and keep tummies moving along.

MEAT & BEANS *(Beans, Beef, Chicken, Eggs, Fish, Nuts, Pork, Tofu)*

- Go lean with protein.
- Choose beans and low-fat versions of protein that are baked, broiled or grilled, not fried.
- Meats and beans supply protein and iron to support muscles and help kids grow.

FATS, OILS & SWEETS *(Butter, Margarine, Oil; Candy, Treats)*

- Go easy on fats, oils and sweets.
- Choose these on occasion, but limit how much and how often kids eat them.
- These extras have lots of calories and fewer nutrients than foods in other food groups.

the doughboy's kitchen clues for kids

DOUGHBOY TIPS: Look for these tidbits throughout the book to show steps that kids can help with, little recipe secrets and menu ideas. And be sure to have kids read the following kitchen safety tips written especially for them.

getting started

- Before you start, always check with an adult to make sure it's a good time to use the kitchen.
- If you have long hair, pull it back to keep it out of your way.
- Always wash hands with soap and dry them before touching any food.
- Read the recipe all the way through before starting. Ask an adult if there is anything you don't understand.
- Before you start, gather all the ingredients and kitchen tools (mixing bowls, measuring cups and spoons, cutting board, scraper) you need for the recipe.
- Measure all the ingredients carefully and double check before you dump them in. Read the recipe again at the end to be sure you haven't left anything out.

finishing up

- Clean up as you go. Put away ingredients, and place used tools in the sink. Wipe up spills when they happen. Don't leave cleaning up to the end.
- Wash tools with warm soapy water. Leave them to drain, or dry them with a clean towel. Put everything away in its proper place.
- Wipe down counters and leave the kitchen neat and clean.

10 ways to play it safe in the kitchen

1 Be sure an adult is in the kitchen before you use a sharp knife, the oven or the microwave.

2 Always dry your hands after washing so your fingers won't be slippery.

3 Wipe up spills right away to avoid slipping.

4 Use a cutting board when slicing or chopping ingredients with a knife.

5 Always use potholders when handling hot dishes to avoid burns.

6 Lift lids away from you and keep your face away from steam.

7 Place large pans on big burners and small pans on small burners. Don't allow handles to stick out over the edge of the stove or another burner.

8 Ask an adult to lift heavy items and help you pour off hot water from heavy pots—as when cooking pasta, for example.

9 Place hot dishes, pots and pans on surfaces that won't be harmed by heat.

10 Read the use-and-care manual before using foil or metal of any kind in the microwave. Use only microwave-safe containers for heating in the microwave.

Blueberry-Bran Pancakes, see page 12

CHAPTER ONE

breakfast

super FAST | blueberry-bran pancakes

prep time: **20 minutes** • start to finish: **20 minutes** • **10 pancakes** (5 inches each)

1 cup Fiber One® original bran cereal

1 egg

1¼ cups buttermilk or milk

2 tablespoons vegetable oil

1 cup all-purpose flour

1 tablespoon sugar

1 teaspoon baking powder

½ teaspoon baking soda

½ teaspoon salt

½ cup fresh or frozen blueberries

Blueberries and/or strawberries, if desired

1 If desired, crush cereal by placing in resealable food-storage plastic bag; seal bag and crush with rolling pin or meat mallet (or crush in food processor). In medium bowl, beat egg with whisk or fork. Beat in buttermilk, oil and cereal; let stand about 5 minutes or until cereal is softened. Beat in remaining ingredients except berries. Gently stir in ½ cup blueberries.

2 Heat skillet or griddle over medium heat, or heat to 375°F. Grease with vegetable oil if necessary (or spray with cooking spray before heating).

3 For each pancake, pour ¼ cup batter into hot skillet (if batter is too thick, stir in additional milk, 1 tablespoon at a time, until as thin as desired). Cook pancakes until puffed and full of bubbles but before bubbles break. Turn; cook other sides until golden brown. Serve topped with blueberries and/or strawberries.

1 PANCAKE: Calories 120; Total Fat 4g (Saturated Fat 0.5g; Trans Fat 0g); Cholesterol 20mg; Sodium 290mg; Total Carbohydrate 18g (Dietary Fiber 3g); Protein 3g EXCHANGES: 1 Starch, 1 Fat CARBOHYDRATE CHOICES: 1

good eats for kids   *The fiber from the cereal in this recipe is important for digestion and, besides, it just adds great flavor. The antioxidant-filled blueberries make a tasty addition.*

substitution idea   *Use raspberries instead of the blueberries. Chopped strawberries would also be good in these pancakes.*

See photo page 10.

super FAST | berry-topped oatmeal pancakes

prep time: **20 minutes** ▪ start to finish: **20 minutes** ▪ **5 servings** (2 pancakes and ¼ cup topping each)

TOPPING

1¼ cups frozen unsweetened mixed berries (from 14-oz bag)

½ cup blueberry syrup

PANCAKES

¾ cup quick-cooking oats

1 tablespoon packed brown sugar

1 cup fat-free (skim) milk

½ teaspoon vanilla

1 egg

1 cup low-fat all-purpose baking mix

1 In 2-quart saucepan, heat topping ingredients over medium heat, stirring occasionally, until berries are thawed and mixture is warm. Remove from heat; set aside.

2 In medium bowl, mix oats, brown sugar, milk and vanilla; set aside.

3 Heat 12-inch nonstick skillet or griddle over medium-high heat, or heat to 375°F. Add egg and baking mix to oat mixture; stir just until all ingredients are moistened.

4 For each pancake, pour slightly less than ¼ cup batter into hot skillet; cook 1 minute to 1 minute 30 seconds or until bubbly. Turn; cook 1 minute longer or until browned. Serve pancakes with topping.

1 SERVING: Calories 280; Total Fat 3.5g (Saturated Fat 0.5g; Trans Fat 0); Cholesterol 45mg; Sodium 270mg; Total Carbohydrate 56g (Dietary Fiber 3g); Protein 6g **EXCHANGES:** ½ Fruit, 1 Starch, 2 Other Carbohydrate, ½ Fat **CARBOHYDRATE CHOICES:** 4

good eats for kids *Everyone will enjoy this power-packed version of pancakes, full of wholesome oatmeal and topped with sweet nutritious fruit.*

scary pancakes

prep time: **30 minutes** ▪ start to finish: **30 minutes** ▪ **8 servings** (1 pancake and 2 tablespoons syrup mixture each)

1 container (6 oz) orange crème low-fat yogurt

¼ cup maple-flavored syrup

2 cups all-purpose baking mix

1¼ cups fat-free (skim) milk

1 egg

1 teaspoon unsweetened baking cocoa

1 teaspoon sugar

1 In small bowl, mix yogurt and syrup until well blended. Set aside.

2 In medium bowl, mix baking mix, milk and egg until well blended. In small bowl, mix 2 tablespoons of the batter, the cocoa and sugar until well blended.

3 Heat 12-inch nonstick skillet or griddle over medium-high heat, or heat to 375°F. Oil hot griddle.

4 For each pancake, drop three ¼- to ½-inch drops of dark batter about 1 to 1½ inches apart into hot skillet, forming eyes and mouth of ghost. Cook about 30 seconds. Immediately pour ¼ cup regular batter; start the pour to cover the "eyes and mouth" and continue the pour downward to form an irregular ghostly shape. Cook 1 to 2 minutes or until pancake is puffed and dry around edges. Turn pancake; cook about 1 minute longer or until other side is golden brown. Serve with syrup mixture.

1 SERVING: Calories 200; Total Fat 6g (Saturated Fat 2g; Trans Fat 0.5g); Cholesterol 30mg; Sodium 470mg; Total Carbohydrate 33g (Dietary Fiber 0g); Protein 5g **EXCHANGES:** 1 Starch, 1½ Other Carbohydrate, 1 Fat **CARBOHYDRATE CHOICES:** 2

DOUGHBOY TIPS

Encourage the kids to design their own scary pancakes on the griddle. Watch them carefully so they're cautious about the heat.

substitution idea *Any flavor of yogurt can be substituted for the orange flavor—choose whatever your kids like.*

pancake banana splits

prep time: **25 minutes** ▪ start to finish: **25 minutes** ▪ **6 servings** (2 pancakes and toppings each)

1 package (16.4-oz) frozen microwave pancakes or buttermilk microwave pancakes (12 pancakes)

3 bananas

1 container (8 oz) strawberry yogurt

1 container (8 oz) vanilla yogurt

1 can (8 oz) crushed pineapple in unsweetened juice, drained

½ cup fresh blueberries

2 tablespoons granola

Fresh strawberries, as desired

1 Microwave pancakes as directed on package. DO NOT OVERHEAT.

2 Cut each banana in half lengthwise and crosswise, making 4 pieces each.

3 To serve, place 2 pancakes on each serving plate. Top each with 2 banana pieces, ⅙ each of strawberry yogurt, vanilla yogurt, pineapple and blueberries. Sprinkle each serving with granola. Garnish with strawberries.

1 SERVING: Calories 340; Total Fat 4.5g (Saturated Fat 1.5g; Trans Fat 0.5g); Cholesterol 10mg; Sodium 350mg; Total Carbohydrate 66g (Dietary Fiber 4g); Protein 9g **EXCHANGES:** 1½ Starch, 1 Fruit, 1½ Other Carbohydrate, ½ Skim Milk, ½ Fat **CARBOHYDRATE CHOICES:** 4½

substitution idea *Turn these into Waffle Banana Splits by using frozen waffles instead of the pancakes. Heat the waffles as directed on the package.*

super FAST | sunny-side up waffles

prep time: **15 minutes** • start to finish: **15 minutes** • **4 waffles**

4 frozen homestyle or
buttermilk waffles

2 containers (6 oz each)
vanilla thick and creamy
low-fat yogurt

4 canned apricot halves,
drained

1 Toast frozen waffles in toaster or toaster oven until warm.
Place on serving plates.

2 Spoon half of 1 container yogurt onto each warm waffle,
spreading to almost completely cover each waffle.

3 Top each waffle with 1 apricot half, rounded side up.

1 WAFFLE: Calories 220; Total Fat 5g (Saturated Fat 1.5g; Trans Fat 1g); Cholesterol 15mg; Sodium 300mg;
Total Carbohydrate 38g (Dietary Fiber 1g); Protein 6g EXCHANGES: 1 Starch, 1½ Other Carbohydrate,
½ Lean Meat, ½ Fat CARBOHYDRATE CHOICES: 2½

substitution idea *Kids will be intrigued because these look
like eggs on waffles—but they are not! Instead of using plain waffles,
mix things up by substituting frozen blueberry or apple-cinnamon
waffles. You could also use peach halves instead of apricot halves.*

super FAST | whole-grain waffles

prep time: **15 minutes** ▪ start to finish: **15 minutes** ▪ **3 servings** (two 4-inch waffles each)

½ cup all-purpose flour

½ cup whole wheat flour

½ cup quick-cooking oats

1 teaspoon baking powder

1¼ cups fat-free (skim) milk

¼ cup fat-free egg product
  or 1 egg

1 tablespoon canola oil

Powdered sugar, if desired

1 Heat nonstick waffle maker. In large bowl, mix all-purpose flour, whole wheat flour, oats and baking powder.

2 In small bowl, mix milk, egg product and oil until well blended. Add to flour mixture all at once; stir just until large lumps disappear.

3 Spread about ⅙ of the batter in hot waffle maker; bake until waffle is golden brown and steaming stops. Repeat to use up batter. Serve sprinkled with powdered sugar.

1 SERVING: Calories 290; Total Fat 6g (Saturated Fat 0.5g; Trans Fat 0g); Cholesterol 0mg; Sodium 250mg; Total Carbohydrate 45g (Dietary Fiber 4g); Protein 13g **EXCHANGES:** 3 Starch, ½ High-Fat Meat **CARBOHYDRATE CHOICES:** 3

good eats for kids *Kids will get a healthy dose of fiber from these waffles. Add some fresh fruit for sweetness and added nutritional value.*

cinnamon-raisin french toast

prep time: **25 minutes** ▪ start to finish: **25 minutes** ▪ **4 servings** (2 slices each)

¾ cup fat-free egg product
   or 3 eggs

¾ cup vanilla soymilk

½ teaspoon vanilla

8 slices whole-grain
   cinnamon-raisin swirl
   bread

Powdered sugar or fresh
   fruit, if desired

1 In medium bowl, beat egg product, soymilk and vanilla with hand beater or whisk until smooth; pour into shallow bowl.

2 Spray 10-inch skillet or griddle with cooking spray; heat skillet over medium heat, or griddle to 375°F. Dip bread into egg mixture until completely soaked. Place in skillet. Cook about 4 minutes on each side or until golden brown. Sprinkle servings with powdered sugar; top with fruit.

1 SERVING: Calories 260; Total Fat 6g (Saturated Fat 1g; Trans Fat 0g); Cholesterol 0mg; Sodium 380mg; Total Carbohydrate 41g (Dietary Fiber 4g); Protein 12g **EXCHANGES:** 2 Starch, ½ Other Carbohydrate, 1 Very Lean Meat, 1 Fat **CARBOHYDRATE CHOICES:** 3

good eats for kids *It's okay to use the whole eggs, but egg substitutes provide the protein from eggs but not the cholesterol found in the yolks. This can be important even for kids.*

peanut butter and banana wraps

prep time: **10 minutes** ▪ start to finish: **10 minutes** ▪ **8 servings**

½ cup reduced-fat creamy peanut butter spread

4 whole wheat or regular flour tortillas (8 to 10 inch)

¼ cup honey

2 small bananas, sliced

¼ cup miniature semisweet chocolate chips, if desired

1 Spread 2 tablespoons of the peanut butter evenly over each tortilla. Drizzle each with 1 tablespoon of the honey. Top with banana slices and chocolate chips.

2 Roll up tortillas; cut each in half. Secure with toothpicks.

1 SERVING: Calories 210; Total Fat 7g (Saturated Fat 1g; Trans Fat 0g); Cholesterol 0mg; Sodium 190mg; Total Carbohydrate 30g (Dietary Fiber 3g); Protein 6g EXCHANGES: 1 Starch, 1 Other Carbohydrate, ½ High-Fat Meat, ½ Fat CARBOHYDRATE CHOICES: 2

DOUGHBOY TIPS

These wraps are perfect for the kids to make themselves. If you want, add some other fruit or jam so they can design their own tasty version.

good eats for kids *Peanut butter, a favorite kid food, contains magnesium, which helps send signals to the muscles via the nervous system.*

banana-oat muffins

prep time: **10 minutes** • start to finish: **30 minutes** • 12 muffins

2 cups Cheerios® cereal

1¼ cups all-purpose flour

⅓ cup packed brown sugar

1 teaspoon baking powder

¾ teaspoon baking soda

1 cup mashed very ripe
 bananas (2 to 3 medium)

⅔ cup fat-free (skim) milk

3 tablespoons vegetable oil

1 egg white

1 Heat oven to 400°F. Spray 12 regular-size muffin cups with cooking spray, or grease bottoms only of muffin cups.

2 Place cereal in resealable food-storage plastic bag; seal bag and crush with rolling pin or meat mallet (or crush in food processor). In large bowl, stir together cereal, flour, brown sugar, baking powder and baking soda. Stir in remaining ingredients just until moistened. Divide batter evenly among muffin cups.

3 Bake 18 to 22 minutes or until golden brown.

1 MUFFIN: Calories 150; Total Fat 4g (Saturated Fat 0.5g; Trans Fat 0g); Cholesterol 0mg; Sodium 170mg; Total Carbohydrate 25g (Dietary Fiber 1g); Protein 3g EXCHANGES: 1 Starch, ½ Other Carbohydrate, ½ Fat CARBOHYDRATE CHOICES: 1½

DOUGHBOY TIPS

For the most yummy banana flavor, make sure the bananas are very ripe before you use them to make these muffins.

good eats for kids   *Kids usually love Cheerios, and because they're made with oats, they're loaded with fiber—the soluble kind that helps to lower blood cholesterol.*

yogurt-bran muffins

prep time: **10 minutes** ▪ start to finish: **30 minutes** ▪ **12 muffins**

1 cup Fiber One original bran cereal

2 egg whites or 1 egg, slightly beaten

¼ cup vegetable oil

2 containers (6 oz each) French vanilla low-fat yogurt

1½ cups all-purpose flour

⅓ cup packed brown sugar

1¼ teaspoons baking soda

½ teaspoon salt

½ cup fresh raspberries or blueberries

1 Heat oven to 400°F. Place paper baking cup in each of 12 regular-size muffin cups, or grease bottom of each muffin cup with shortening. Place cereal in resealable food-storage plastic bag; seal bag and crush with rolling pin or meat mallet (or crush in food processor).

2 In medium bowl, stir together egg whites, oil and yogurt. Add cereal, flour, brown sugar, baking soda and salt; stir just until dry ingredients are moistened. Gently stir in berries. Divide batter evenly among muffin cups, filling each ¾ full.

3 Bake 18 to 20 minutes or until golden brown. Immediately remove from pan.

1 MUFFIN: Calories 170; Total Fat 5g (Saturated Fat 1g; Trans Fat 0g); Cholesterol 0mg; Sodium 270mg; Total Carbohydrate 28g (Dietary Fiber 3g); Protein 3g **EXCHANGES:** 1 Starch, 1 Other Carbohydrate, 1 Fat **CARBOHYDRATE CHOICES:** 2

good eats for kids *Yogurt adds calcium and a touch of vanilla to these easy muffins.*

breakfast-to-go

prep time: **10 minutes** ▪ start to finish: **25 minutes** ▪ **21 servings** (⅓ cup each)

¼ cup sugar

½ teaspoon ground cinnamon

⅓ cup butter or margarine

1 cup Corn Chex® cereal

1 cup Rice Chex® cereal

1 cup Wheat Chex® cereal

1 cup Honey Nut Cheerios® cereal

¾ cup toasted sliced almonds

1 cup dried banana chips

½ cup dried blueberries or raisins

1 In small bowl, mix sugar and cinnamon.

2 In large microwavable bowl, microwave butter uncovered on High about 40 seconds or until melted. Stir in cereals and almonds until evenly coated. Microwave uncovered on High 2 minutes, stirring after 1 minute.

3 Stir in sugar mixture and banana chips until evenly coated. Microwave uncovered on High 1 minute. Spread on paper towels to cool, about 15 minutes. Place in serving bowl; stir in blueberries. Store in airtight container.

1 SERVING: Calories 130; Total Fat 7g (Saturated Fat 3g; Trans Fat 0g); Cholesterol 10mg; Sodium 80mg; Total Carbohydrate 15g (Dietary Fiber 1g); Protein 2g **EXCHANGES:** ½ Starch, ½ Other Carbohydrate, 1½ Fat **CARBOHYDRATE CHOICES:** 1

oven directions   *Heat oven to 300°F. In small bowl, mix sugar and cinnamon. In ungreased 13 × 9-inch pan, melt butter in oven. Stir in cereals and almonds until evenly coated. Bake uncovered 15 minutes. Stir in sugar mixture and banana chips until evenly coated; bake 15 minutes longer. Spread on paper towels to cool, about 15 minutes. Place in serving bowl; stir in blueberries. Store in airtight container.*

good eats for kids   *Here's a great way to have kids in a hurry eat something wholesome and delicious. You can layer the mix with their favorite yogurt in a disposable covered container for a parfait-to-go.*

make any morning special!

Breakfast—it seems like creativity in the morning is not always an option. But it's considered the most important meal of the day, so why not think ahead and plan to serve some yummy new combinations using that old famous favorite—cereal! Your kids will look at morning in a new way when you try any of these great ideas.

Mix 2 favorite cereals like Cheerios and Honey Nut Cheerios, then top with fruit such as:

- Fresh strawberries
- Fresh blueberries
- Fresh raspberries

- Sliced fresh bananas
- Sliced fresh peaches or nectarines

Or, try one of the following combinations:

- Top fat-free or low-fat yogurt with Banana Nut Cheerios and thawed frozen fruit.

- Top cold or hot cereal with mixed dried fruit.
- Try any cereal with soymilk.
- Stir dried cranberries into oatmeal and drizzle with a little maple syrup.
- Stir golden raisins into oatmeal and sprinkle with a little brown sugar.
- Walnuts or pecans plus a drizzle of honey make great toppings for cream of wheat.

super FAST | creamy apple-raisin oatmeal

prep time: **10 minutes** ▪ start to finish: **10 minutes** ▪ **1 serving** (¾ cup)

⅓ cup quick-cooking oats

1 tablespoon raisins

⅔ cup apple juice

2 tablespoons French vanilla low-fat yogurt (from 6-oz container)

2 teaspoons packed brown sugar, if desired

1 In 2-cup microwavable cereal bowl, stir oats, raisins and apple juice until well blended.

2 Microwave on High 1½ to 2 minutes, stirring every 30 seconds, until thickened. Top with yogurt; sprinkle with brown sugar.

1 SERVING: Calories 240; Total Fat 2g (Saturated Fat 0.5g; Trans Fat 0); Cholesterol 0mg; Sodium 100mg; Total Carbohydrate 49g (Dietary Fiber 3g); Protein 5g **EXCHANGES:** 2 Starch, 1½ Fruit **CARBOHYDRATE CHOICES:** 3

DOUGHBOY TIPS

This is a good recipe for the kids to help make. Need more servings? It's easy to double or triple the ingredients and make individual bowls.

good eats for kids   *Warm wholesome oatmeal is a great day starter as it contains soluble fiber, which can help reduce blood cholesterol levels. This yummy breakfast will appeal to kids with added sweetness from the juice, raisins and brown sugar. You could also add a crunchy slice of apple after microwaving.*

veggie and swiss cheese omelet

prep time: **25 minutes** • start to finish: **25 minutes** • 2 servings

FILLING

¼ cup sliced (¼-inch-thick) zucchini

¼ cup thinly sliced onion

¼ cup chopped red bell pepper (¼ medium)

¼ cup chopped yellow or green bell pepper (¼ medium)

¼ cup sliced fresh mushrooms

¼ teaspoon salt

Dash pepper

OMELET

1 carton (8 oz) fat-free egg product (1 cup) or 4 eggs

1 tablespoon fat-free (skim) milk

TOPPINGS

¼ cup shredded reduced-fat Swiss cheese (1 oz)

1 small plum (Roma) tomato, sliced

1 Cut zucchini slices into quarters. Heat 8- to 10-inch nonstick skillet with sloping sides (omelet pan) over medium heat. Add zucchini and remaining filling ingredients; cook 4 to 6 minutes, stirring occasionally, until tender. Remove cooked vegetables from skillet; place on plate and cover to keep warm. Cool skillet 1 minute; wipe clean with paper towel.

2 In small bowl, mix omelet ingredients. Heat same skillet over medium heat. Pour egg mixture into skillet; cook 4 to 5 minutes without stirring, but lifting edges occasionally to allow uncooked egg mixture to flow to bottom of skillet, until mixture is set but top is still moist.

3 Spoon cooked vegetables onto half of omelet; sprinkle with cheese. With wide spatula, loosen edge of omelet and fold over vegetables. Arrange tomato slices on top of omelet.

1 SERVING: Calories 120; Total Fat 1g (Saturated Fat 0.5g; Trans Fat 0g); Cholesterol 5mg; Sodium 550mg; Total Carbohydrate 9g (Dietary Fiber 2g); Protein 17g **EXCHANGES:** 1½ Vegetable, 2 Very Lean Meat **CARBOHYDRATE CHOICES:** ½

good eats for kids   *This is a great way for kids to have veggies in the morning. The red, yellow, and green bell peppers are high in vitamin C, and all the vegetables offer some fiber.*

substitution idea   *Feel free to change the cheese. We like the Swiss, but if your family prefers, mozzarella, Cheddar and Colby are all good choices.*

egg 'n bell pepper scramble

prep time: **10 minutes** ▪ start to finish: **10 minutes** ▪ **4 servings** (½ cup each)

1 cup frozen bell pepper and onion stir-fry (from 1-lb bag), coarsely chopped

1½ cups fat-free egg product or 6 eggs

¼ teaspoon salt

⅛ teaspoon pepper

1 medium plum (Roma) tomato, seeded, chopped

¼ cup crumbled feta cheese with garlic and herbs (2 oz)

1 Heat 10-inch nonstick skillet over medium-high heat. Add bell pepper and onion stir-fry; cook 2 to 3 minutes, stirring frequently, until vegetables are crisp-tender.

2 Meanwhile, in medium bowl, beat egg product, salt and pepper. Pour egg mixture over vegetables in skillet. Reduce heat to medium; cook 4 to 6 minutes, stirring frequently, until eggs are set but still moist.

3 Divide egg mixture evenly onto 4 serving plates; top each with tomato and cheese.

1 SERVING: Calories 100; Total Fat 3.5g (Saturated Fat 2g; Trans Fat 0g); Cholesterol 15mg; Sodium 480mg; Total Carbohydrate 6g (Dietary Fiber 1g); Protein 12g **EXCHANGES:** ½ Vegetable, 1½ Very Lean Meat, ½ Fat **CARBOHYDRATE CHOICES:** ½

substitution idea *Using the fat-free egg product keeps the fat and cholesterol low in this easy scramble, but you can use the whole eggs if you choose. If your kids don't like feta cheese, use a little grated Parmesan instead.*

spring veggie frittata

prep time: **20 minutes** ▪ start to finish: **20 minutes** ▪ 4 servings

4 teaspoons olive oil

½ lb fresh asparagus spears, trimmed, cut into 1-inch pieces

1 small red bell pepper, thinly sliced

2 cartons (8 oz each) fat-free egg product (2 cups) or 8 eggs, lightly beaten

1 tablespoon finely chopped fresh basil

¼ teaspoon salt

1 In 10-inch nonstick skillet, heat 2 teaspoons of the oil over medium-high heat. Add asparagus and bell pepper; cook 3 to 5 minutes, stirring frequently, until crisp-tender. Remove from heat; place cooked vegetables in medium bowl. Stir egg product, basil and salt into vegetables.

2 In same skillet, add remaining 2 teaspoons oil and the egg mixture. Cook over medium heat about 5 minutes or until bottom is lightly browned and top is set, lifting edges occasionally to allow uncooked egg mixture to flow to bottom of skillet.

3 Place skillet-size heatproof plate, upside down, on top of skillet. Turn plate and skillet over; slide frittata back into skillet, browned side up. Cook until bottom is lightly browned. Turn upside down onto serving plate if desired. Cut into wedges.

1 SERVING: Calories 80; Total Fat 4.5g (Saturated Fat 0.5g; Trans Fat 0g); Cholesterol 0mg; Sodium 260mg; Total Carbohydrate 4g (Dietary Fiber 1g); Protein 7g **EXCHANGES:** ½ Other Carbohydrate, 1 Lean Meat **CARBOHYDRATE CHOICES:** 0

substitution idea   *Kids don't like asparagus? Why not use broccoli florets or even green beans instead? Either one will cook in about the same time as the asparagus.*

eggs 'n spinach on english muffins

prep time: **15 minutes** ▪ start to finish: **15 minutes** ▪ **2 servings**

¼ cup plain fat-free yogurt

1 tablespoon fat-free mayonnaise

½ teaspoon Dijon mustard

2 eggs

1 English muffin, split, toasted

½ cup fresh baby spinach leaves

Dash pepper

1 In small microwavable bowl, mix yogurt, mayonnaise and mustard. Microwave on High 20 to 40 seconds or until warm. Stir; set aside.

2 In 10-inch skillet, heat 1½ to 2 inches water to boiling. Reduce heat to medium-low. Break each egg into shallow dish; carefully slide egg into hot water. Quickly spoon hot water over each egg until film forms over yolk. Simmer 3 to 5 minutes or until eggs are desired doneness.

3 Meanwhile, spread about 2 tablespoons sauce on each English muffin half. Top each with half of the spinach leaves.

4 With slotted spoon, remove eggs from water; place on top of spinach. Top each with half of remaining sauce; sprinkle with pepper.

1 SERVING: Calories 170; Total Fat 6g (Saturated Fat 2g; Trans Fat 0g); Cholesterol 215mg; Sodium 310mg; Total Carbohydrate 17g (Dietary Fiber 1g); Protein 11g **EXCHANGES:** 1 Starch, 1 Medium-Fat Meat **CARBOHYDRATE CHOICES:** 1

DOUGHBOY TIPS

Have one of the kids toast the muffin while the eggs are cooking. It's also fun for them to watch the eggs as they poach.

good eats for kids   *Spinach is an excellent source of the important nutrients folic acid and vitamin C. This leafy green is also a good source of iron.*

mexican breakfast wraps

prep time: **20 minutes** ▪ start to finish: **20 minutes** ▪ **4 servings**

1 large green bell pepper, chopped (1 cup)

1 large onion, chopped (1 cup)

1¾ cups fat-free egg product (from two 8-oz cartons)

⅓ cup fat-free (skim) milk

¼ teaspoon salt

⅛ teaspoon pepper

4 fat-free flour tortillas (8 to 10 inch)

½ cup shredded fat-free Cheddar cheese (2 oz)

¼ cup chunky-style salsa

1 Spray 10-inch skillet with cooking spray; heat over medium heat. Add bell pepper and onion; cover and cook 4 to 6 minutes, stirring occasionally, until tender.

2 In medium bowl, mix egg product, milk, salt and pepper until well blended. Spray vegetables and skillet with cooking spray. Pour egg product mixture over vegetables; cook until set, occasionally stirring gently.

3 Meanwhile, heat tortillas as directed on package.

4 To serve, place warm tortillas on 4 individual plates. Spoon scrambled egg mixture down center of each tortilla. Top each with cheese and salsa. Roll up tortillas.

1 SERVING: Calories 160; Total Fat 5g (Saturated Fat 3g; Trans Fat 0g); Cholesterol 15mg; Sodium 570mg; Total Carbohydrate 12g (Dietary Fiber 2g); Protein 16g **EXCHANGES:** ½ Starch, 1 Vegetable, 1½ Very Lean Meat, 1 Fat **CARBOHYDRATE CHOICES:** 1

DOUGHBOY TIPS

Let the kids roll up the tortillas with the eggs inside. Then serve with cubes of cantaloupe and orange juice.

good eats for kids *Eggs are a source of choline, a vitamin-like substance necessary in the making of a neurotransmitter called acetylcholine, which helps send nerve impulses from cell to cell.*

super FAST | yummy strawberry-banana smoothies

prep time: **10 minutes** ▪ start to finish: **10 minutes** ▪ **3 servings** (1 cup each)

2 cups strawberry or strawberry banana low-fat yogurt (from 2-lb container)

¼ cup orange juice

1 cup frozen whole strawberries, slightly thawed

1 banana, cut into chunks

2 teaspoons miniature semisweet chocolate chips or slightly crushed Trix® cereal

1 In blender, place all ingredients except chocolate chips. Cover; blend on high speed about 30 seconds or until smooth and thick.

2 Pour into 3 glasses; sprinkle with chocolate chips or crushed cereal. Serve immediately.

1 SERVING: Calories 280; Total Fat 2g (Saturated Fat 1g; Trans Fat 0g); Cholesterol 0mg; Sodium 80mg; Total Carbohydrate 61g (Dietary Fiber 3g); Protein 5g **EXCHANGES:** 1 Fruit, 2 Other Carbohydrate, 1 Skim Milk **CARBOHYDRATE CHOICES:** 4

DOUGHBOY TIPS

Kids can help to microwave the strawberries for quick thawing. Have them check every 15 seconds so the strawberries are just barely thawed.

good eats for kids *Nutrition-packed smoothies like these are a great way to include calcium and a variety of vitamins in a single delicious morning beverage. They're also a great choice for a snack any time of the day.*

super FAST | blueberry-pomegranate smoothies

prep time: **5 minutes** ▪ start to finish: **5 minutes** ▪ **2 servings** (¾ cup each)

1 cup frozen blueberries

½ cup pomegranate juice

½ cup soy milk

1 In blender, place ingredients. Cover; blend on high speed about 1 minute or until smooth.

2 Pour into 2 glasses. Serve immediately.

1 SERVING: Calories 140; Total Fat 2g (Saturated Fat 0g; Trans Fat 0g); Cholesterol 0mg; Sodium 40mg; Total Carbohydrate 28g (Dietary Fiber 4g); Protein 3g **EXCHANGES**: 1 Starch, 1 Fruit **CARBOHYDRATE CHOICES**: 2

DOUGHBOY TIPS

Let the kids put all of the yummy ingredients in the blender. Then show them how to cover and blend— a great kitchen lesson!

good eats for kids   *First-prize blueberries are great for kids and adults because they contain antioxidants that may help protect healthy body cells from oxygen damage.*

super FAST | honey nut-peach smoothies

prep time: **5 minutes** • start to finish: **5 minutes** • **4 servings** (1 cup each)

1⅓ cups harvest peach or vanilla low-fat yogurt (from 2-lb container)

1½ cups Honey Nut Cheerios cereal

1 can (15 oz) sliced peaches in juice, drained

1 cup fat-free (skim) milk

1 banana, sliced

⅛ teaspoon ground cinnamon, if desired

1 In blender, place ingredients. Cover; blend on high speed 10 seconds. Scrape down sides of blender. Cover; blend about 20 seconds longer or until smooth.

2 Pour into 4 glasses. Serve immediately.

1 SERVING: Calories 220; Total Fat 2.5g (Saturated Fat 1g; Trans Fat 0g); Cholesterol 5mg; Sodium 160mg; Total Carbohydrate 42g (Dietary Fiber 2g); Protein 6g **EXCHANGES:** ½ Starch, 1 Fruit, 1 Other Carbohydrate, ½ Skim Milk, ½ Fat **CARBOHYDRATE CHOICES:** 3

good eats for kids   *Fruits such as peaches provide vitamin C along with fiber and great taste—all great things for growing kids!*

substitution idea   *For frostier smoothies, use 1⅓ cups frozen sliced peaches, slightly thawed, instead of the canned peaches.*

super FAST | frozen yogurt smoothies

prep time: **10 minutes** • start to finish: **10 minutes** • **2 servings** (1 cup each)

1 ripe banana, peeled, cut into chunks

1 ripe nectarine, peeled, pitted and quartered

4 to 5 large fresh strawberries, cut in half

1 cup strawberry low-fat frozen yogurt

1 In blender or food processor, place ingredients. Cover; blend on high speed 20 to 30 seconds or until smooth.

2 Pour into 2 glasses. Serve immediately.

1 SERVING: Calories 240; Total Fat 2.5g (Saturated Fat 1.5g; Trans Fat 0g); Cholesterol 5mg; Sodium 75mg; Total Carbohydrate 48g (Dietary Fiber 3g); Protein 7g **EXCHANGES:** 1½ Fruit, 1 Other Carbohydrate, 1 Skim Milk **CARBOHYDRATE CHOICES:** 3

good eats for kids   *Add a little more fiber to these smoothies by adding 1 tablespoon wheat germ or Fiber One cereal to the blender before blending.*

substitution idea   *Do you have some ripe peaches? Use 1 as a perfect substitute for the nectarine. Also, a few fresh raspberries and frozen raspberry yogurt can be used in place of the strawberries and strawberry yogurt.*

super FAST | breakfast parfait for one

prep time: **10 minutes** ▪ start to finish: **10 minutes** ▪ **1 serving**

⅓ cup Whole Grain Total® cereal

1 container (6 oz) low-fat yogurt (any fruit flavor)

½ cup blueberries, sliced strawberries and/or raspberries

1 Place cereal in resealable food-storage plastic bag; seal bag and crush with rolling pin or meat mallet (or crush in food processor).

2 In tall narrow glass, place ⅓ of the yogurt. Top with ⅓ of the cereal and ⅓ of the fruit. Repeat layers twice.

1 SERVING: Calories 220; Total Fat 1g (Saturated Fat 0g; Trans Fat 0g); Cholesterol 0mg; Sodium 125mg; Total Carbohydrate 45g (Dietary Fiber 3g); Protein 7g **EXCHANGES:** 1 Starch, ½ Fruit, 1 Other Carbohydrate, ½ Skim Milk **CARBOHYDRATE CHOICES:** 3

good eats for kids *It's easy to stuff a lot of nutritional value in a dessert-like breakfast when you use this favorite cereal plus yogurt and fruit.*

substitution idea *You can make this breakfast any way you like. Use your child's favorite flavor of yogurt along with berries and fruits in season.*

tropical banana nut parfaits

prep time: **15 minutes** ▪ start to finish: **15 minutes** ▪ **4 servings**

1½ cups strawberry low-fat yogurt (from 32-oz container)

2 cups Banana Nut Cheerios® cereal

1 medium banana, sliced

1 cup sliced fresh strawberries

2 tablespoons coconut, toasted*

1 In each of 4 parfait glasses, alternate layers of yogurt, cereal, banana and strawberries.

2 Top each serving with coconut. Serve immediately.

1 SERVING: Calories 200; Total Fat 2.5g (Saturated Fat 1.5g; Trans Fat 0g); Cholesterol 0mg; Sodium 160mg; Total Carbohydrate 41g (Dietary Fiber 2g); Protein 4g **EXCHANGES:** 1 Starch, ½ Fruit, 1 Other Carbohydrate, ½ Fat **CARBOHYDRATE CHOICES:** 3

To toast coconut quickly in the microwave, spread it in a shallow microwavable bowl or pie plate. Microwave uncovered on High 1 minute to 1 minute 30 seconds, stirring every 30 seconds, until golden brown.

substitution idea *If your kids don't like coconut, substitute a few miniature chocolate chips instead.*

super FAST | ambrosia yogurt parfaits

prep time: **10 minutes** ▪ start to finish: **10 minutes** ▪ **4 servings**

3 containers (6 oz each) French vanilla low-fat yogurt

1 can (8 oz) crushed pineapple in juice, drained

2 cups Honey Nut Cheerios cereal

1 medium banana, sliced (1 cup)

1 can (11 oz) mandarin orange segments in light syrup, drained

¼ cup coconut, toasted*

4 fresh strawberries, sliced

1 In medium bowl, mix yogurt and pineapple. Into each of 4 parfait glasses, place ¼ cup of the cereal.

2 Spoon 2 tablespoons yogurt mixture on top of cereal in each glass. Top each with ¼ cup cereal, then with ¼ of the banana slices.

3 Spoon 2 tablespoons yogurt mixture onto banana in each; top each with orange segments. Spoon remaining yogurt mixture over orange segments. Sprinkle with coconut. Garnish with strawberries.

1 SERVING: Calories 310; Total Fat 4g (Saturated Fat 2.5g; Trans Fat 0g); Cholesterol 10mg; Sodium 200mg; Total Carbohydrate 62g (Dietary Fiber 4g); Protein 7g EXCHANGES: 1 Starch, 1 Fruit, 1½ Other Carbohydrate, ½ Skim Milk, ½ Fat CARBOHYDRATE CHOICES: 4

*To toast coconut quickly in the microwave, spread it in a shallow microwavable bowl or pie plate. Microwave uncovered on High 1 minute to 1 minute 30 seconds, stirring every 30 seconds, until golden brown.

good eats for kids   *Turn these pretty parfaits into fun for the kids by letting them build their own. They'll love eating their cereal in this tasty way.*

Italian Beef Dippers, see page 61

lunch

turkey sandwich wedges

prep time: **10 minutes** ▪ start to finish: **10 minutes** ▪ **6 servings**

1 package (12 oz) cheese or garlic focaccia bread (8 to 10 inch)

3 cups torn romaine lettuce

9 oz cooked turkey, cut into bite-size strips (2 cups)

⅓ cup reduced-fat creamy Caesar or ranch dressing

¼ cup grated Parmesan cheese

¼ teaspoon coarse ground black pepper

1 Cut focaccia bread in half horizontally; set aside.

2 In large bowl, mix remaining ingredients.

3 Spoon turkey mixture evenly onto bottom half of bread. Cover with top half of bread. Cut into 6 wedges to serve.

1 SERVING: Calories 290 (Calories from Fat 90); Total Fat 10g (Saturated Fat 2.5g, Trans Fat 0g); Cholesterol 45mg; Sodium 720mg; Total Carbohydrate 30g (Dietary Fiber 1g) **% DAILY VALUE:** Vitamin A 30%; Vitamin C 10%; Calcium 8%; Iron 15% **EXCHANGES:** 1½ Starch, ½ Other Carbohydrate, 2 Lean Meat, ½ Fat **CARBOHYDRATE CHOICES:** 2

substitution idea: *Chicken would be great instead of the turkey in these fun wedge-shaped sandwiches. Also, substitute any other lettuce variety that you might have on hand.*

super FAST | bean and veggie wraps

prep time: **15 minutes** ▪ start to finish: **15 minutes** ▪ **4 servings**

- 4 low-fat whole wheat tortillas or flour tortillas (6 to 8 inch)
- 1 medium onion, cut lengthwise in half, then cut crosswise into thin slices
- 1 can (15 oz) black beans, drained, rinsed
- 1 jar (4.5 oz) sliced mushrooms, drained
- 4 cups loosely packed fresh spinach
- ½ cup shredded reduced-fat Cheddar cheese (2 oz)

1 Heat tortillas as directed on package.

2 Meanwhile, spray 10-inch skillet with cooking spray; heat over medium heat. Add onion; cook about 3 minutes, stirring frequently, until onion is crisp-tender. Stir in beans and mushrooms; cook until heated through. Stir in spinach; remove from heat.

3 Spoon ¼ of the bean mixture down center of each tortilla. Sprinkle with cheese. Fold one end of each tortilla up about 1 inch over filling; fold right and left sides over folded end, overlapping. Fold remaining end down.

1 SERVING: Calories 250; Total Fat 3g (Saturated Fat 1g, Trans Fat 0g); Cholesterol 0mg; Sodium 720mg; Total Carbohydrate 42g (Dietary Fiber 12g); Protein 14g EXCHANGES: 2½ Starch, 1 Vegetable, ½ Medium-Fat Meat CARBOHYDRATE CHOICES: 3

 DOUGHBOY TIPS

Fresh spinach is "fluffy". Be sure to lightly pack the leaves when measuring. If you're buying spinach by weight, 1 cup of fresh spinach is about 1½ ounces.

super FAST | chicken and apple pockets

prep time: **15 minutes** ▪ start to finish: **15 minutes** ▪ **6 sandwiches**

3 tablespoons mayonnaise or salad dressing

3 tablespoons plain fat-free yogurt

⅛ teaspoon seasoned salt

1 cup chopped cooked chicken breast

1 medium tart-sweet red apple, cored, cut into bite-size pieces (about ¾ cup)

3 tablespoons thinly sliced celery

6 whole wheat or white mini pita (pocket) breads

1 In medium bowl, mix mayonnaise, yogurt and seasoned salt. Gently stir in chicken, apple and celery to coat.

2 Cut slit in side of each pita bread to open and form pocket. Fill each with ⅓ cup chicken mixture.

1 SANDWICH: Calories 230; Total Fat 8g (Saturated Fat 1.5g, Trans Fat 0g); Cholesterol 20mg; Sodium 330mg; Total Carbohydrate 28g (Dietary Fiber 4g); Protein 12g **EXCHANGES:** 1½ Starch, ½ Other Carbohydrate, 1 Very Lean Meat, 1 Fat **CARBOHYDRATE CHOICES:** 2

good eats for kids   *A recipe made with mayonnaise and yogurt instead of just mayonnaise will be lower in fat and still have great taste.*

chicken caesar pitas

prep time: **30 minutes** ▪ start to finish: **30 minutes** ▪ **4 servings**

- 2 boneless skinless chicken breasts (about 4 oz each)
- ⅓ cup reduced-fat Caesar dressing
- ⅛ teaspoon pepper
- 2 cups coarsely chopped romaine lettuce
- ¼ cup shredded carrot (1 small carrot)
- 2 tablespoons shredded Parmesan cheese
- 2 whole wheat pita (pocket) breads (6 inch), cut in half to form pockets
- 1 plum (Roma) tomato, thinly sliced

1 Set oven control to broil. Brush both sides of chicken with 1 tablespoon of the dressing; sprinkle with pepper.

2 Place chicken on rack in broiler pan. Broil with tops 4 to 6 inches from heat 12 to 15 minutes, turning once, until juice of chicken is clear when center of thickest part is cut (170°F). Cool about 5 minutes. Cut into thin slices.

3 In medium bowl, toss lettuce, carrot and cheese with remaining dressing until coated. Fill each pita bread half with tomato and chicken; top with lettuce mixture.

1 SERVING: Calories 220; Total Fat 7g (Saturated Fat 2g; Trans Fat 0g); Cholesterol 45mg; Sodium 480mg; Total Carbohydrate 22g (Dietary Fiber 3g); Protein 18g EXCHANGES: 1 Starch, ½ Vegetable, 2 Lean Meat CARBOHYDRATE CHOICES: 1½

substitution idea *Spinach is a nice substitute for the romaine, or mix spinach and romaine instead.*

super FAST | garden-fresh tuna salad sandwiches

prep time: **15 minutes** ▪ start to finish: **15 minutes** ▪ **4 sandwiches**

1 (6-oz.) can water-packed tuna, drained, flaked

⅔ cup chopped seeded cucumber

½ cup shredded carrot

¼ cup chopped green onions

¼ cup fat-free mayonnaise or salad dressing

2 tablespoons nonfat sour cream

1 tablespoon lemon juice

4 leaves leaf lettuce

8 slices whole wheat bread, toasted if desired

1 In medium bowl, combine all ingredients except lettuce and bread; mix well.

2 Place 1 lettuce leaf on each of 4 slices of bread; spoon and spread ½ cup tuna mixture onto each. Top with remaining slices of bread.

1 SANDWICH: Calories 210; Total Fat 2.5g (Saturated Fat 1g; Trans Fat 0g); Cholesterol 15mg; Sodium 540mg; Total Carbohydrate 29g (Dietary Fiber 5g); Protein 18g **EXCHANGES:** 1 Starch, ½ Other Carbohydrate, 1 Vegetable, 2 Very Lean Meat **CARBOHYDRATE CHOICES:** 2

super FAST | mediterranean turkey bagelwiches

prep time: **5 minutes** ▪ start to finish: **5 minutes** ▪ 2 sandwiches

2 tablespoons hummus (from 5-oz container)

2 bagels, split

3 oz sliced smoked turkey

½ medium cucumber, thinly sliced

½ small red onion, thinly sliced

8 spinach leaves

1 Spread about 1 tablespoon hummus on bottom half of each bagel.

2 Layer turkey, cucumber, onion and spinach on bottom half of each bagel. Top with remaining bagel halves.

1 SANDWICH: Calories 310; Total Fat 6g (Saturated Fat 1g; Trans Fat 0g); Cholesterol 25mg; Sodium 1130mg; Total Carbohydrate 44g (Dietary Fiber 6g); Protein 21g EXCHANGES: 2½ Starch, 1 Vegetable, 1½ Lean Meat CARBOHYDRATE CHOICES: 3

DOUGHBOY TIPS

Bagels are perfect to pack in lunches as they hold their shape until lunchtime. Cut each sandwich into fourths for easy eating.

substitution idea *If your kids already like hummus, try introducing a new variety such as roasted garlic or red pepper hummus. Look for different flavors in your grocer's refrigerated case.*

swiss apple bagelwiches

prep time: **20 minutes** ▪ start to finish: **20 minutes** ▪ **4 sandwiches**

2 oz ⅓-less-fat cream cheese (Neufchâtel), softened

1 teaspoon Dijon mustard

1 teaspoon chopped fresh chives or ½ teaspoon freeze-dried chopped chives

2 whole wheat or pumpernickel bagels, split, toasted

1 apple

2 (7×½-inch) slices wafer-thin low-sodium reduced-fat Swiss cheese, each cut in half

1 Heat oven to 350°F. In small bowl, mix cream cheese, mustard and chives; blend well. Spread on cut sides of bagels. Place on ungreased cookie sheet.

2 Core apple; cut into ½-inch-thick rings. Place 1 apple ring on each bagel half; top each with piece of cheese.

3 Bake 5 to 6 minutes or until cheese is melted and sandwiches are warm.

1 SANDWICH: Calories 230; Total Fat 4g (Saturated Fat 2g; Trans Fat 0g); Cholesterol 10mg; Sodium 260mg; Total Carbohydrate 41g (Dietary Fiber 3g); Protein 7g EXCHANGES: 2 Starch, ½ Other Carbohydrate, ½ Fat CARBOHYDRATE CHOICES: 3

substitution idea *We really like the whole wheat or pumpernickel bagels for these sandwiches, but you could use any flavor that your family likes. Why not try cinnamon-raisin, onion or sesame seed bagels instead?*

lunches to write home about

It's a tall order to come up with lunch ideas that kids will actually eat and are good for them. Youngsters can be pretty stubborn when it comes to what they like and will eat. So here's a bunch of good-for-you lunch ideas that even the pickiest eaters will be able to choose from.

For sandwiches:

- Vary the bread—try whole wheat slices, pita bread halves or whole wheat flour tortillas.
- Cut sandwiches into cute shapes with cookie cutters.
- Look for low-fat cheese slices like mozzarella, Swiss and Cheddar.
- Use lean meats like turkey, chicken and ham.
- Hummus makes a great sandwich filling.
- Place lettuce between meat and low-fat mayonnaise or mustard so it doesn't get soggy.

Other things to pack:

- Whole grain pasta salad with veggies—use low-fat Italian dressing
- Tabbouleh salad
- Pickles
- Baby carrots
- Canned tuna, chicken or salmon with whole grain crackers
- Fat-free or low-fat yogurt
- Fruit of all kinds—bananas, strawberries, grapes, orange segments, blueberries, melon cubes
- Individual containers of applesauce
- Individual containers of sugar-free fruit-flavored gelatin

open-faced veggie burger melts

prep time: **20 minutes** ▪ start to finish: **20 minutes** ▪ **2 open-faced sandwiches**

2 meatless original soy protein burgers (from 9-oz box)

4 medium fresh broccoli spears (about 2½ oz)

¼ cup water

2 slices whole-grain bread, toasted

2 teaspoons sweet honey mustard

2 tomato slices

2 slices Swiss cheese (¾ oz each), cut into 6 strips

1 Cook frozen protein burgers as directed on box.

2 Meanwhile, in small microwavable bowl, place broccoli and water; cover with microwavable plastic wrap. Microwave on High 2 to 3 minutes or until broccoli is crisp-tender; drain.

3 Set oven control to broil. Place toasted bread slices on ungreased cookie sheet; spread each with mustard. Place protein burgers on bread; top with tomato slices and broccoli. Arrange cheese slices on top of broccoli.

4 Broil with tops 3 to 4 inches from heat 1 to 2 minutes or until cheese is melted.

1 OPEN-FACED SANDWICH: Calories 260; Total Fat 8g (Saturated Fat 4g; Trans Fat 0g); Cholesterol 20mg; Sodium 490mg; Total Carbohydrate 23g (Dietary Fiber 7g); Protein 23g EXCHANGES: 1 Starch, 1½ Vegetable, 2½ Lean Meat CARBOHYDRATE CHOICES: 1½

good eats for kids *Soy protein burgers contain almost 75% less fat than ground beef. The broccoli and tomato in these hearty sandwiches add important nutrients, including vitamin C.*

italian beef dippers

prep time: **30 minutes** ▪ start to finish: **30 minutes** ▪ **6 servings** (1 sandwich and ⅓ cup soup each)

1 can (18.5 oz) ready-to-
serve French onion soup

½ teaspoon Italian
seasoning

¾ lb thinly sliced cooked
roast beef

6 crusty French rolls
(each 3 to 4 inches long)

6 slices (½ oz each)
provolone cheese

1 In 2-quart saucepan, heat soup and Italian seasoning over
medium heat, stirring occasionally, until hot. Add beef. Heat
4 to 6 minutes, stirring occasionally, until hot.

2 Using serrated knife, cut rolls in half lengthwise. Remove beef
from soup. Arrange beef on bottom halves of rolls.

3 Cut each slice of cheese into 2 pieces. Put 2 pieces of cheese on
top of beef on each sandwich. Cover with top halves of rolls.

4 Divide soup evenly among 6 soup bowls. Serve sandwiches with
warm soup for dipping.

1 SERVING: Calories 260; Total Fat 7g (Saturated Fat 3.5g; Trans Fat 0g); Cholesterol 40mg; Sodium 1320mg;
Total Carbohydrate 30g (Dietary Fiber 1g); Protein 20g **EXCHANGES:** 2 Starch, 2 Lean Meat **CARBOHYDRATE
CHOICES:** 2

DOUGHBOY TIPS

*After the filling is heated, have the kids help assemble
the sandwiches. While they're working, explain that
French people describe these sandwiches as "with
juice." Then tell them the French term is spelled a-u j-u-s
and is pronounced "oh zhoo," and let the fun begin!*

See photo on page 48.

super FAST | chunky pizza soup

prep time: **15 minutes** ▪ start to finish: **15 minutes** ▪ **4 servings** (1¼ cups each)

1 can (19 oz) ready-to-serve tomato rotini soup

1 can (14.5 oz) no-salt-added diced tomatoes with basil, garlic and oregano, undrained

3 slices Canadian bacon, chopped

½ cup croutons

¼ cup shredded mozzarella cheese (1 oz)

1 In 2-quart saucepan, heat soup, tomatoes and Canadian bacon to boiling, stirring occasionally. Reduce heat to low; simmer 5 minutes.

2 Divide croutons evenly among 4 soup bowls. Pour soup over croutons. Sprinkle each serving with 1 tablespoon cheese.

1 SERVING: Calories 130; Total Fat 3.5g (Saturated Fat 1.5g; Trans Fat 0g); Cholesterol 15mg; Sodium 780mg; Total Carbohydrate 16g (Dietary Fiber 2g); Protein 8g **EXCHANGES:** ½ Starch, 1 Vegetable, ½ Lean Meat, ½ Fat CARBOHYDRATE CHOICES: 1

DOUGHBOY TIPS

Kids can make this soup in the microwave. Just mix the soup, tomatoes and Canadian bacon in a microwavable bowl. Microwave on High 5 to 7 minutes or until hot, stirring after 3 minutes.

substitution idea *Do your kids have a favorite pizza meat topping? Try it in this soup. Cooked Italian sausage, cooked ground or roast beef, or pepperoni are all good substitutions for the Canadian bacon.*

bean and barley vegetable soup

prep time: **30 minutes** • start to finish: **30 minutes** • **4 servings** (1¾ cups each)

2 teaspoons olive oil

2 cups ready-to-eat
baby-cut carrots, thinly
sliced

2 medium celery stalks,
thinly sliced (about 1 cup)

1 medium onion, chopped
(½ cup)

½ cup uncooked quick-
cooking barley

1 can (15.5 oz) great
northern beans, drained,
rinsed

1 can (14.5 oz) diced
tomatoes with basil, garlic
and oregano, undrained

1 can (8 oz) no-salt-added
tomato sauce

2½ cups water

1 In 3-quart saucepan, heat oil over medium-high heat. Add carrots, celery and onion; cook 3 minutes, stirring frequently, until vegetables are crisp-tender.

2 Stir in remaining ingredients. Heat to boiling. Reduce heat to medium; cover and cook 15 to 20 minutes, stirring occasionally, until vegetables and barley are tender.

1 SERVING: Calories 300; Total Fat 3.5g (Saturated Fat 0.5g; Trans Fat 0g); Cholesterol 0mg; Sodium 220mg; Total Carbohydrate 55g (Dietary Fiber 13g); Protein 11g **EXCHANGES:** 3 Starch, 2 Vegetable, ½ Fat **CARBOHYDRATE CHOICES:** 3½

good eats for kids   *This hearty soup is a great choice for lunch. It's filled with wholesome goodness from barley, beans and lots of veggies.*

super FAST | hearty ham and vegetable soup

prep time: **20 minutes** • start to finish: **20 minutes** • **5 servings** (1 cup each)

1 can (19 oz) ready-to-serve hearty tomato soup

1 can (15 or 16 oz) pork and beans in tomato sauce

1 cup diced reduced-sodium cooked ham

1 cup frozen mixed vegetables

1 In 2-quart saucepan, heat ingredients to boiling over medium-high heat, stirring occasionally.

2 Reduce heat to medium-low; simmer uncovered 10 minutes, stirring occasionally, until vegetables are tender.

1 SERVING: Calories 200; Total Fat 3g (Saturated Fat 0.5g; Trans Fat 0g); Cholesterol 20mg; Sodium 1080mg; Total Carbohydrate 31g (Dietary Fiber 7g); Protein 12g **EXCHANGES:** 1 Starch, ½ Other Carbohydrate, 1 Vegetable, 1 Lean Meat **CARBOHYDRATE CHOICES:** 2

substitution idea   *Mixed veggies are usually a favorite with kids, but you could use cut green beans, sliced carrots or corn instead.*

zesty mexican soup

prep time: **30 minutes** ▪ start to finish: **30 minutes** ▪ **6 servings** (1 cup each)

2 cups cubed cooked chicken

1 can (14 oz) reduced-sodium chicken broth

1 bottle (12 oz) low-sodium vegetable juice

1 can (11 oz) whole kernel corn with red and green peppers, undrained

1 cup chunky-style salsa

1 can (4.5 oz) chopped green chiles, drained

¼ cup chopped fresh cilantro

1 In 4-quart saucepan, heat all ingredients except cilantro to boiling, stirring frequently.

2 Reduce heat; simmer about 10 minutes, stirring occasionally, until hot. Stir in cilantro.

1 SERVING: Calories 160; Total Fat 3.5g (Saturated Fat 1g; Trans Fat 0g); Cholesterol 40mg; Sodium 770mg; Total Carbohydrate 17g (Dietary Fiber 1g); Protein 15g EXCHANGES: 1 Starch, ½ Vegetable, 1½ Lean Meat CARBOHYDRATE CHOICES: 1

good eats for kids *Healthful vegetable juice is a blend of tomato, carrot, celery, beet, parsley, lettuce, watercress and spinach juices. What a great way to add vegetable value to this soup that's perfect for kids!*

southwestern turkey chili soup

prep time: **30 minutes** ▪ start to finish: **30 minutes** ▪ **6 (1⅓-cup) servings**

½ lb fresh ground turkey breast

1 (15.5-oz.) can light or dark red kidney beans, drained, rinsed

1 (14.5-oz.) can salsa tomatoes diced with green chiles

1 (8-oz.) can tomato sauce

4 cups water

3 teaspoons beef-flavor instant bouillon

½ teaspoon chili powder

¼ teaspoon cumin

1 In large saucepan, brown ground turkey. Add all remaining ingredients; mix well. Bring to a boil.

2 Reduce heat to low; simmer 15 to 20 minutes, stirring occasionally.

1 SERVING: Calories 140; Total Fat 1g (Saturated Fat 0g, Trans Fat 0g); Cholesterol 25mg; Sodium 820mg; Total Carbohydrate 17g (Dietary Fiber 4g); Protein 14g **EXCHANGES:** 1 Starch, ½ Vegetable, 1½ Very Lean Meat, 1 Lean Meat **CARBOHYDRATE CHOICES:** 1

substitution idea *If desired, Mexican stewed tomatoes or any spicy tomatoes can be substituted for the salsa tomatoes.*

chunky tomato chicken soup

prep time: **25 minutes** ▪ start to finish: **25 minutes** ▪ **3 servings** (1⅓ cups each)

2 teaspoons olive oil

½ lb chicken breast strips for stir-fry

½ cup sliced leeks

1 can (14.5 oz) diced tomatoes with basil, garlic and oregano, undrained

1¾ cups reduced-sodium chicken broth (from 32-oz carton)

2 oz uncooked angel hair pasta (capellini), broken

Shredded Parmesan cheese, if desired

1 In 3-quart saucepan, heat oil over medium-high heat until hot. Add chicken and leeks; cook 5 minutes, stirring frequently.

2 Stir in tomatoes and broth. Heat to boiling. Reduce heat; simmer 10 minutes.

3 Add pasta; simmer 3 to 5 minutes or until pasta is tender and chicken is no longer pink in center. Serve with cheese.

1 SERVING: Calories 250; Total Fat 6g (Saturated Fat 1g; Trans Fat 0g); Cholesterol 45mg; Sodium 570mg; Total Carbohydrate 25g (Dietary Fiber 2g); Protein 23g **EXCHANGES:** 1½ Starch, 1 Vegetable, 2 Lean Meat **CARBOHYDRATE CHOICES:** 1½

substitution idea *Got some leftover chicken to use up? Go ahead and substitute it for the strips here. Or, use cooked turkey pieces instead.*

chicken and barley soup

prep time: **10 minutes** ▪ start to finish: **30 minutes** ▪ **6 servings** (1⅓ cups each)

1 carton (32 oz) reduced-sodium chicken broth (4 cups)

1 can (14.5 oz) diced tomatoes, undrained

2 medium carrots, sliced (1 cup)

2 medium stalks celery, sliced (1 cup)

1 cup sliced fresh mushrooms (about 3 oz)

⅓ cup uncooked quick-cooking barley

1 teaspoon dried minced onion

2 cups chopped deli rotisserie chicken (from 2- to 2½-lb chicken)

1 In 3-quart saucepan, mix all ingredients except chicken. Heat to boiling over medium-high heat, stirring occasionally. Reduce heat to medium. Cover; simmer 15 to 20 minutes or until barley is tender.

2 Add chicken. Cover; cook about 3 minutes or until chicken is hot.

1 SERVING: Calories 160; Total Fat 3.5g (Saturated Fat 1g; Trans Fat 0g); Cholesterol 40mg; Sodium 700mg; Total Carbohydrate 15g (Dietary Fiber 3g); Protein 17g **EXCHANGES:** ½ Starch, 1½ Vegetable, 1½ Lean Meat CARBOHYDRATE CHOICES: 1

DOUGHBOY TIPS

Be sure to use quick-cooking barley because the regular type needs to cook longer than this recipe allows.

easy a-b-c soup

prep time: **5 minutes** ▪ start to finish: **20 minutes** ▪ **10 servings** (1¼ cups each)

2 cups cubed cooked chicken or turkey

2 cups frozen mixed vegetables

½ cup chopped celery

¼ cup chopped onion

¼ teaspoon dried thyme leaves

1 bay leaf

6 cups reduced-sodium chicken broth (from two 32-oz cartons)

1 cup uncooked alphabet macaroni

Salt and pepper, if desired

1 In 4-quart saucepan or Dutch oven, mix all ingredients except macaroni. Heat to boiling, stirring occasionally. Reduce heat; stir in macaroni.

2 Simmer 12 to 15 minutes or until vegetables and macaroni are tender. Remove bay leaf. Season to taste with salt and pepper.

1 SERVING: Calories 140; Total Fat 2.5g (Saturated Fat 0.5g; Trans Fat 0g); Cholesterol 25mg; Sodium 370mg; Total Carbohydrate 17g (Dietary Fiber 2g); Protein 13g **EXCHANGES:** 1 Starch, ½ Vegetable, 1 Lean Meat CARBOHYDRATE CHOICES: 1

 DOUGHBOY TIPS

Serve this soup for lunch and it's the perfect opportunity to practice the alphabet with the kids.

super FAST | mac 'n cheese with broccoli

prep time: **10 minutes** ▪ start to finish: **10 minutes** ▪ **3 servings** (⅔ cup each)

½ cup uncooked elbow macaroni (2 oz)

1 box (10 oz) frozen broccoli in a zesty cheese sauce

1 In 2-quart saucepan, cook macaroni as directed on package. Drain; return to saucepan.

2 Meanwhile, cook broccoli as directed on box.

3 Stir broccoli with cheese sauce into macaroni.

1 SERVING: Calories 130; Total Fat 2.5g (Saturated Fat 0g; Trans Fat 0g); Cholesterol 0mg; Sodium 380mg; Total Carbohydrate 22g (Dietary Fiber 2g); Protein 4g **EXCHANGES:** 1 Starch, 1 Vegetable, ½ Fat **CARBOHYDRATE CHOICES:** 1½

good eats for kids *Here's a great way to get kids to eat their broccoli. Adding this veggie to the classic combo of mac 'n cheese provides a nutrient boost with extra vitamins A and C, and fiber.*

mini pizzas

prep time: **20 minutes** ▪ start to finish: **30 minutes** ▪ 20 pizzas

1 can (13.8 oz) refrigerated classic pizza crust or 1 can (11 oz) refrigerated thin pizza crust

⅓ cup basil pesto

20 slices plum (Roma) tomatoes

1 cup shredded mozzarella cheese (4 oz)

1 If using classic crust: Heat oven to 425°F. If using thin crust: Heat oven to 400°F.

2 Spray or grease cookie sheet. Unroll dough on work surface. Press dough into 12×8-inch rectangle. With round cutter, cut dough into 20 rounds; place rounds 1 inch apart on cookie sheet. Spread each with pesto. Top each with 1 tomato slice. Sprinkle with cheese.

3 Bake classic crust 10 to 12 minutes, thin crust 8 to 10 minutes, or until cheese is melted.

1 PIZZA: Calories 90; Total Fat 4g (Saturated Fat 1.5g; Trans Fat 0g); Cholesterol 0mg; Sodium 210mg; Total Carbohydrate 10g (Dietary Fiber 0g); Protein 3g **EXCHANGES:** ½ Starch, 1 Fat **CARBOHYDRATE CHOICES:** ½

DOUGHBOY TIPS

Always be sure to keep the refrigerated dough very cold until just before you are ready to shape it.

substitution idea   *Let kids top their own mini pizzas with favorite pizza toppings, such as cooked Italian sausage, pepperoni or just simply cheese.*

spanish chicken pizza

prep time: **15 minutes** ▪ start to finish: **30 minutes** ▪ **6 servings**

1 package (10 oz) prebaked thin Italian pizza crust (12 inch)

1 cup diced cooked chicken breast

1 cup shredded mozzarella cheese (4 oz)

3 medium plum (Roma) tomatoes, sliced

½ cup quartered artichoke hearts (from 14-oz can), drained, coarsely chopped

3 medium pimiento-stuffed green olives, sliced

1 Heat oven to 450°F. On ungreased cookie sheet, place pizza crust; sprinkle chicken evenly over crust. Sprinkle with ⅔ cup of the cheese.

2 Arrange tomato slices over cheese. Top with artichokes and olives; sprinkle with remaining ⅓ cup cheese.

3 Bake 10 to 12 minutes or until cheese is melted and pizza is hot.

1 SERVING: Calories 240; Total Fat 8g (Saturated Fat 3g; Trans Fat 0g); Cholesterol 30mg; Sodium 400mg; Total Carbohydrate 26g (Dietary Fiber 2g); Protein 15g **EXCHANGES:** 1½ Starch, ½ Vegetable, 1½ Lean Meat, ½ Fat **CARBOHYDRATE CHOICES:** 2

good eats for kids   *Chicken breast is a lower fat, tasty alternative to pepperoni as a pizza topping, and kids usually like it.*

super FAST | shake-it-up salad

prep time: **15 minutes** • start to finish: **15 minutes** • **1 serving**

2 tablespoons low-fat
French dressing

¼ cup cubed cooked chicken

2 tablespoons shredded
Cheddar cheese

2 tablespoons grated carrot

1 cup torn salad greens

1 Measure ingredients into plastic container with tight-fitting lid. Cover container tightly. Refrigerate until ready to serve.

2 Just before serving, shake to toss all ingredients.

1 SERVING: Calories 210; Total Fat 12g (Saturated Fat 4.5g; Trans Fat 0g); Cholesterol 45mg; Sodium 480mg; Total Carbohydrate 13g (Dietary Fiber 2g); Protein 14g EXCHANGES: 2 Vegetable, 1½ Lean Meat, 1½ Fat CARBOHYDRATE CHOICES: 1

substitution idea *You can make this salad different every time. If French isn't your kids' favorite, any dressing will be just as tasty. Also, turkey is a good substitute for the chicken, and you can use any cheese your kids like.*

Pizza Chicken and Ravioli, see page 90

CHAPTER THREE

dinner

balsamic-glazed chicken breasts

prep time: **35 minutes** ▪ start to finish: **30 minutes** ▪ **4 servings**

GLAZE

⅓ cup packed brown sugar

⅓ cup balsamic vinegar

1 teaspoon chopped fresh
    rosemary leaves

1 teaspoon finely chopped
    garlic

CHICKEN

4 bone-in skin-on chicken
    breasts (8 oz each)

½ teaspoon salt

¼ teaspoon pepper

1 Heat gas or charcoal grill. In small bowl, mix glaze ingredients; set aside.

2 Sprinkle chicken with salt and pepper. Place chicken on grill, skin side down. Cover grill; cook 10 minutes over medium heat. Turn chicken; brush half the glaze evenly over chicken. Continue cooking and brushing with remaining glaze 10 to 12 minutes longer or until juice of chicken is clear when thickest part is cut to bone (170°F).

1 SERVING: Calories 310; Total Fat 9g (Saturated Fat 2.5g; Trans Fat 0g); Cholesterol 95mg; Sodium 380mg; Total Carbohydrate 22g (Dietary Fiber 0g); Protein 34g EXCHANGES: 1 Other Carbohydrate, 4½ Lean Meat CARBOHYDRATE CHOICES: 1½

substitution idea   *Substitute any fresh herb, such as thyme, oregano, tarragon or Italian parsley, for the rosemary in this recipe.*

pineapple-glazed chicken breasts with couscous pilaf

prep time: **25 minutes** ▪ start to finish: **25 minutes** ▪ 4 servings

PILAF

¼ cup finely chopped red bell pepper

¼ teaspoon chicken-flavor instant bouillon

1½ cups water

1 cup uncooked couscous

¼ cup sliced green onions (4 medium)

CHICKEN

4 boneless skinless chicken breasts (about 1¼ lb)

⅓ cup pineapple preserves

1 tablespoon sweet hot mustard

1 tablespoon water

Additional sliced green onions, if desired

1 In 2-quart saucepan, heat bell pepper, bouillon and 1½ cups water to boiling over high heat. Remove from heat; stir in couscous. Cover; let stand 5 minutes. Stir in onions; set aside; transfer half of mixture to medium microwavable bowl.

2 Meanwhile, set oven control to broil. Line broiler pan with foil; spray with cooking spray. Place chicken breasts on pan. Broil with tops 4 to 6 inches from heat 5 minutes. In small bowl, mix preserves and mustard; transfer half of mixture to small microwavable bowl.

3 Turn chicken. Brush chicken with half of preserves mixture; discard any remaining. Broil 3 to 5 minutes longer or until juice of chicken is clear when center of thickest part is cut (170°F).

4 Stir couscous mixture lightly with fork; divide evenly among 4 serving plates. Top each with chicken. Stir 1 tablespoon water into remaining preserves mixture. Microwave on High 20 to 40 seconds or until warm; spoon over chicken. Garnish with additional sliced green onions.

1 SERVING: Calories 380; Total Fat 4.5g (Saturated Fat 1g; Trans Fat 0g); Cholesterol 75mg; Sodium 180mg; Total Carbohydrate 53g (Dietary Fiber 3g); Protein 32g **EXCHANGES:** 2½ Starch, 1 Other Carbohydrate, 3½ Very Lean Meat **CARBOHYDRATE CHOICES:** 3½

DOUGHBOY TIPS

If the kids have never had couscous, explain that it's just a different form of pasta for them to try. Chances are, they'll really like it, especially with a little of the sweet sauce.

orange-glazed chicken with rosemary

prep time: **30 minutes** ▪ start to finish: **30 minutes** ▪ 4 servings

2 teaspoons canola or
   olive oil

4 boneless skinless chicken
   breasts (about 1¼ lb)

¼ cup orange juice

¾ cup reduced-sodium
   chicken broth (from
   32-oz carton)

1 teaspoon chopped
   fresh or ½ teaspoon
   dried rosemary leaves,
   crumbled

⅛ teaspoon coarse ground
   black pepper

2 teaspoons Dijon mustard

1 naval orange, peeled,
   thinly sliced

Fresh rosemary sprigs,
   if desired

1 In 12-inch nonstick skillet, heat oil over medium-high heat. Add chicken; cook 3 to 5 minutes, turning once, until browned on both sides.

2 Add orange juice and ½ cup of the chicken broth to chicken in skillet; sprinkle with rosemary and pepper. Cover; reduce heat to medium. Cook 12 to 15 minutes or until juice of chicken is clear when center of thickest part is cut (170°F). Place chicken on serving platter.

3 Add remaining ¼ cup chicken broth and mustard to skillet; increase heat to high. Heat to boiling. Boil 4 to 5 minutes, stirring frequently, until mixture is glaze consistency. Stir in orange slices; cook 1 to 2 minutes, stirring constantly, just until heated.

4 Spoon glaze over chicken on platter. Garnish with fresh rosemary sprigs.

1 SERVING: Calories 180; Total Fat 6g (Saturated Fat 1g; Trans Fat 0g); Cholesterol 70mg; Sodium 230mg; Total Carbohydrate 6g (Dietary Fiber 0g); Protein 26g **EXCHANGES:** ½ Other Carbohydrate, 3½ Very Lean Meat, ½ Fat **CARBOHYDRATE CHOICES:** ½

good eats for kids *Chicken contains vitamin B_6, important for digesting proteins and helping to keep hair and nerves healthy. Plus, chicken breasts are fairly low in fat—good for both kids and adults.*

super FAST | ultimate barbecue-rubbed chicken

prep time: **20 minutes** ▪ start to finish: **20 minutes** ▪ **4 servings**

1 tablespoon packed brown sugar

2 teaspoons smoked Spanish paprika

½ teaspoon ground cumin

¼ teaspoon garlic salt

¼ teaspoon ancho chili powder

4 boneless skinless chicken breasts (about 1¼ lb)

½ cup barbecue sauce, warmed, if desired

1 Heat gas or charcoal grill. In small bowl, mix brown sugar, paprika, cumin, garlic salt and chili powder. Rub both sides of chicken with seasoning mixture.

2 Place chicken on grill. Cover grill; cook over medium heat 8 to 10 minutes, turning once, until juice of chicken is clear when center of thickest part is cut (170°F).

3 Serve chicken with barbecue sauce.

1 SERVING: Calories 210; Total Fat 4g (Saturated Fat 1g; Trans Fat 0g); Cholesterol 75mg; Sodium 460mg; Total Carbohydrate 17g (Dietary Fiber 0g); Protein 27g **EXCHANGES:** 1 Other Carbohydrate, 3 Lean Meat **CARBOHYDRATE CHOICES:** 1

substitution idea *If smoked Spanish paprika is unavailable, substitute any variety of paprika, such as sweet and mild or even hot. Either will provide the aromatic flavor from the peppers without the smokiness.*

chicken blt wraps

prep time: **15 minutes** ▪ start to finish: **15 minutes** ▪ **8 servings** (½ wrap each)

AIOLI

¼ cup reduced-fat mayonnaise or salad dressing

1 large clove garlic, finely chopped

1 tablespoon fresh lemon juice

WRAPS

4 flour tortillas (10 inch)

8 leaves green leaf lettuce

1 package (9 oz) thinly sliced oven-roasted chicken breast

2 medium tomatoes, chopped

¼ cup bacon flavor bits or chips

1 In small bowl, beat aioli ingredients with whisk. Spread on each tortilla, leaving 2-inch border at bottom of each.

2 Arrange 2 lettuce leaves on each tortilla, leaving 2-inch border at bottom. Evenly top each with chicken, tomatoes and bacon bits.

3 Fold bottom edge of each tortilla up, and roll tightly. To serve, cut each wrap in half. Secure, if desired, with toothpick, foil or waxed paper.

1 SERVING: Calories 190; Total Fat 7g (Saturated Fat 1.5g; Trans Fat 0.5g); Cholesterol 20mg; Sodium 700mg; Total Carbohydrate 22g (Dietary Fiber 2g); Protein 10g EXCHANGES: 1 Starch, 1 Vegetable, ½ Lean Meat, 1 Fat CARBOHYDRATE CHOICES: 1½

DOUGHBOY TIPS

You and the kids can roll these up ahead of time. Then wrap each half in plastic wrap and store in the refrigerator. They make a great quick meal when time is short or you're all on the run.

pizza chicken and ravioli

prep time: **30 minutes** · start to finish: **30 minutes** · **4 servings** (1⅓ cups each)

1 package (9 oz) refrigerated cheese-filled ravioli

1 jar (2.5 oz) sliced mushrooms, drained

1 can (14.5 oz) reduced-sodium diced tomatoes with onion and green pepper, undrained

1 can (8 oz) pizza sauce

1 package (9 oz) frozen cooked chicken breast strips (2 cups)

1 Cook and drain ravioli as directed on package. Return ravioli to saucepan.

2 Add remaining ingredients; stir well.

3 Heat over medium-high heat about 5 minutes, stirring frequently, until hot.

1 SERVING: Calories 350; Total Fat 10g (Saturated Fat 5g; Trans Fat 0g); Cholesterol 75mg; Sodium 800mg; Total Carbohydrate 38g (Dietary Fiber 3g); Protein 26g EXCHANGES: 2 Starch, 1½ Vegetable, 2½ Lean Meat, ½ Fat CARBOHYDRATE CHOICES: 2½

DOUGHBOY TIPS

Refrigerated ravioli comes with all sorts of fillings. The next time you're grocery shopping with the kids, let them choose their favorite kind to use in this recipe.

See photo on page 80.

chicken and broccoli-parmesan pasta

prep time: **30 minutes** ▪ start to finish: **30 minutes** ▪ **6 servings**

8 oz uncooked whole wheat or multigrain penne pasta (about 2½ cups)

3 cups fresh broccoli florets

1 lb boneless skinless chicken breasts, cut into bite-size pieces

1 teaspoon adobo seasoning

2 tablespoons olive oil

1 clove garlic, minced

¼ cup light mayonnaise

⅛ teaspoon black pepper

2 tablespoons shaved Parmesan cheese

1 In Dutch oven, cook pasta as directed on package, adding broccoli during last 5 minutes of cooking time. Drain well. Return to hot Dutch oven.

2 Meanwhile, in medium bowl, combine chicken pieces and adobo seasoning; toss to coat. In large skillet, heat oil over medium-high heat. Add garlic; cook and stir 30 seconds. Add chicken; cook 3 to 4 minutes or until chicken is no longer pink in center, stirring occasionally.

3 Add chicken to drained pasta and broccoli in Dutch oven. Stir in mayonnaise and pepper. Cook over low heat until heated through, stirring occasionally.

4 To serve, sprinkle with Parmesan cheese.

1 SERVING: Calories 320; Total Fat 10g (Saturated Fat 1.5g, Trans Fat 0g); Cholesterol 50mg; Sodium 380mg; Total Carbohydrate 33g (Dietary Fiber 3g); Protein 24g **EXCHANGES:** 2 Starch, ½ Vegetable, 2½ Very Lean Meat, 1 Fat **CARBOHYDRATE CHOICES:** 2

super FAST asian turkey patties

prep time: **20 minutes** • start to finish: **20 minutes** • 6 servings

1 lb lean ground turkey breast

½ cup chopped fresh mushrooms

¼ cup chopped green onions (4 medium)

¼ cup finely chopped red bell pepper (¼ medium)

2 tablespoons reduced-sodium soy sauce

1 teaspoon chopped garlic in water (from 4.5-oz jar)

1 tablespoon teriyaki baste and glaze (from 12-oz bottle)

1 Heat closed contact grill 5 minutes.

2 Meanwhile, in large bowl, mix all ingredients except teriyaki baste and glaze. Shape mixture into 6 patties, ½ inch thick.

3 When grill is heated, place patties on bottom grill surface. Close grill; cook 8 to 10 minutes or until thermometer inserted in center of patties reads 165°F.

4 Spread ½ teaspoon teriyaki baste and glaze on each patty.

1 SERVING: Calories 110; Total Fat 4g (Saturated Fat 1g; Trans Fat 0g); Cholesterol 50mg; Sodium 340mg; Total Carbohydrate 2g (Dietary Fiber 0g); Protein 16g EXCHANGES: 2½ Very Lean Meat, ½ Fat CARBOHYDRATE CHOICES: 0

good eats for kids *Lean ground turkey breast has about ⅛ the fat per 4-ounce serving compared to regular ground turkey. For best results, use lean ground turkey breast for this recipe.*

lemony turkey primavera skillet

prep time: **30 minutes** • start to finish: **30 minutes** • **6 servings** (1½ cups each)

5 oz uncooked bow-tie (farfalle) pasta (1½ cups)

½ lb fresh asparagus spears, trimmed, cut into 1½-inch pieces (about 2 cups)

6 oz fresh ready-to-eat baby-cut carrots, halved lengthwise (1⅓ cups)

1 cup reduced-fat chicken broth (from 32-oz carton)

4 teaspoons cornstarch

½ teaspoon garlic-pepper blend

1 lb fresh turkey breast slices, cut into thin bite-size strips

1 cup fresh whole mushrooms, quartered

1 can (14 oz) baby corn cobs, drained, rinsed

1 teaspoon grated lemon peel

Salt and pepper, if desired

1 In Dutch oven or 4-quart saucepan, cook pasta to desired doneness as directed on package, adding asparagus and carrots during last 2 to 4 minutes of cooking time. Cook until asparagus is crisp-tender. Drain.

2 Meanwhile, in small bowl, mix broth, cornstarch and garlic-pepper blend. Set aside.

3 Spray 12-inch skillet with cooking spray. Heat over medium-high heat until hot. Add turkey and mushrooms; cook 3 to 5 minutes, stirring frequently, until turkey is lightly browned and no longer pink in center.

4 Add broth mixture; cook and stir just until mixture begins to thicken. Add cooked pasta and vegetables, corn and lemon peel; cook and stir until hot. Season with salt and pepper to taste.

1 SERVING: Calories 260; Total Fat 2g (Saturated Fat 0g; Trans Fat 0g); Cholesterol 50mg; Sodium 460mg; Total Carbohydrate 37g (Dietary Fiber 3g); Protein 24g EXCHANGES: 2 Starch, 2 Vegetable, 2 Very Lean Meat CARBOHYDRATE CHOICES: 2½

good eats for kids *Turkey breast is a lean protein that supplies amino acids, which give structure to the body in skin, cell membranes and muscles. The best part, though, is that kids usually like it and will eat it!*

substitution idea *One pound of boneless skinless chicken breast can be used in place of the turkey breast slices in this recipe.*

turkey clubhouse salad

prep time: **15 minutes** • start to finish: **15 minutes** • **6 servings**

DRESSING
⅓ cup chopped fresh chives

⅓ cup reduced-fat mayonnaise

⅓ cup buttermilk

¼ teaspoon salt

⅛ teaspoon pepper

SALAD
6 slices purchased precooked bacon or ¼ cup real bacon pieces

1 bag (10 oz) chopped romaine lettuce

1½ cups cubed cooked turkey breast (about ½ lb)

2 medium tomatoes, cut into thin wedges

1 In small bowl, mix dressing ingredients. Set aside.

2 If using bacon slices, heat as directed on package until crisp. Drain on paper towels; crumble.

3 In large bowl, mix lettuce and turkey. Pour dressing over salad; toss gently to coat. Arrange salad on serving platter. Arrange tomatoes and bacon over top.

1 SERVING: Calories 140; Total Fat 6g (Saturated Fat 2g; Trans Fat 0g); Cholesterol 45mg; Sodium 500mg; Total Carbohydrate 7g (Dietary Fiber 1g); Protein 15g EXCHANGES: 1½ Vegetable, 1½ Medium-Fat Meat CARBOHYDRATE CHOICES: ½

DOUGHBOY TIPS

Breadsticks go great with this main-dish salad, and they're easy and fun for kids to make. Let them create their own shapes from the dough.

substitution idea *Chicken is a great substitute for the turkey if you have it on hand. Also, we've used reduced-fat mayonnaise, but you could use fat-free mayo instead.*

asian chicken salads with peanuts

prep time: **20 minutes** ▪ start to finish: **20 minutes** ▪ **4 servings**

1 lb uncooked chicken breast strips for stir-frying

¾ cup Oriental dressing and marinade

2 teaspoons vegetable oil

3 cups thinly sliced Chinese (napa) cabbage

3 cups fresh baby spinach leaves

¼ cup sliced green onions (4 medium)

2 tablespoons coarsely chopped dry-roasted peanuts

Additional dressing, if desired

1 In medium bowl, mix chicken and ¼ cup of the dressing; toss to coat. Let stand at room temperature 10 minutes to marinate.

2 In 8-inch nonstick skillet, heat oil over medium-high heat until hot. Remove chicken from marinade with slotted spoon and add to skillet; discard remaining marinade. Cook and stir chicken 4 to 6 minutes or until browned and no longer pink in center. Remove from heat. Add remaining ½ cup dressing; stir to mix.

3 Divide cabbage and spinach evenly among 4 serving plates. Top with chicken mixture. Sprinkle with onions and peanuts. Serve with additional dressing.

1 SERVING: Calories 200; Total Fat 8g (Saturated Fat 2g; Trans Fat 0g); Cholesterol 70mg; Sodium 600mg; Total Carbohydrate 3g (Dietary Fiber 1g); Protein 28g EXCHANGES: 1 Vegetable, 3 Lean Meat CARBOHYDRATE CHOICES: 0

substitution idea *If you prefer, shredded iceberg or romaine lettuce can be used in place of the Chinese cabbage.*

skillet fish with quick corn relish

prep time: **15 minutes** ▪ start to finish: **15 minutes** ▪ **4 servings**

RELISH

1 can (11 oz) whole kernel corn with red and green peppers, drained, rinsed

2 tablespoons sliced green onions (2 medium)

2 tablespoons chopped fresh cilantro

½ teaspoon ground cumin

1 tablespoon lime juice

1 teaspoon honey

FISH

¼ teaspoon ground cumin

⅛ teaspoon pepper

4 cod or halibut fillets (1 lb)

1 In medium bowl, mix relish ingredients; set aside.

2 In small bowl, mix ¼ teaspoon cumin and the pepper; sprinkle on both sides of each fish fillet.

3 Heat 12-inch nonstick skillet over medium-high heat. Add fish; cook 5 to 8 minutes, turning once, until fish flakes easily with fork. Serve fish with relish.

1 SERVING: Calories 180; Total Fat 2g (Saturated Fat 0g; Trans Fat 0g); Cholesterol 60mg; Sodium 320mg; Total Carbohydrate 18g (Dietary Fiber 1g); Protein 23g **EXCHANGES:** 1 Starch, 3 Very Lean Meat CARBOHYDRATE CHOICES: 1

DOUGHBOY TIPS

Get the ingredients ready for the relish, then let the youngsters mix it together. If they don't like cilantro, it's okay to leave it out.

good eats for kids   *Fish is an excellent source of protein and is low in saturated fat. Plus, mild fish like the cod or halibut in this recipe are often favored by kids.*

super FAST | tuna noodle skillet

prep time: **20 minutes** ▪ start to finish: **20 minutes** ▪ **6 servings** (1 cup each)

3½ cups mini lasagna (mafalda) noodles (8 oz)

1 cup chopped celery (1½ to 2 stalks)

2 tablespoons water

½ cup reduced-fat sour cream

½ cup reduced-fat ranch dressing

1 can (12 oz) tuna in water, drained, flaked

1 jar (2 oz) chopped pimientos, drained

1 Cook and drain noodles as directed on package.

2 Meanwhile, in 12-inch nonstick skillet, place celery and water. Cover; cook over medium heat 3 to 4 minutes or until celery is crisp-tender.

3 Gently stir in cooked noodles and remaining ingredients. Cook about 5 minutes, stirring frequently, until hot.

1 SERVING: Calories 300; Total Fat 6g (Saturated Fat 2g; Trans Fat 0g); Cholesterol 30mg; Sodium 400mg; Total Carbohydrate 38g (Dietary Fiber 2g); Protein 21g EXCHANGES: 2½ Starch, 2 Very Lean Meat, ½ Fat CARBOHYDRATE CHOICES: 2½

substitution idea   *You can adjust this to suit the tastes of your family. Some kids just don't care for celery, so it's easy to omit. Then add some frozen peas instead, or even coarsely chopped fresh carrot is a good option. The mini lasagna noodles are fun, but if you have rotini on hand, you can use it instead.*

parmesan-crusted fish

prep time: **10 minutes** • start to finish: **25 minutes** • 4 servings

1 lb halibut, cod, haddock
   or other firm-texture fish
   fillets (about ¾ inch thick),
   cut into 4 serving pieces

2 tablespoons reduced-fat
   mayonnaise

½ teaspoon finely grated
   lemon peel

⅛ teaspoon pepper

2 tablespoons Italian-style
   dry bread crumbs

2 tablespoons grated
   Parmesan cheese

Lemon wedges, if desired

1 Heat oven to 450°F. Line 15×10×1-inch pan with foil; spray with cooking spray. Place fish fillets in pan.

2 In small bowl, stir mayonnaise, lemon peel and pepper until blended. Spread over top of each fillet. In another small bowl, mix bread crumbs and Parmesan cheese. Spoon evenly over mayonnaise mixture; pat crumb mixture lightly into mayonnaise.

3 Bake 12 to 15 minutes or until fish flakes easily with fork. Serve with lemon wedges.

1 SERVING: Calories 150; Total Fat 5g (Saturated Fat 1.5g, Trans Fat 0g); Cholesterol 65mg; Sodium 260mg; Total Carbohydrate 3g (Dietary Fiber 0g); Protein 23g **EXCHANGES:** 3 Very Lean Meat, 1 Fat **CARBOHYDRATE CHOICES:** 0

pineapple shrimp stir-fry

prep time: **25 minutes** ▪ start to finish: **25 minutes** ▪ **4 servings** (1 cup each)

1 lb uncooked deveined peeled medium shrimp, thawed if frozen, tail shells removed

½ teaspoon salt

¼ teaspoon pepper

1 cup julienne (matchstick-cut) carrots

1 medium red bell pepper, cut into 1-inch pieces

1 can (8 oz) pineapple chunks, drained

⅔ cup sweet-and-sour sauce

Hot cooked rice, if desired

1 Heat nonstick wok or 12-inch nonstick skillet over medium-high heat. Add shrimp; sprinkle with salt and pepper. Cook and stir 1 minute. Add carrots and bell pepper; cook and stir 2 to 3 minutes or until shrimp are pink, and vegetables are crisp-tender.

2 Add pineapple chunks and sweet-and-sour sauce; cook and stir 2 to 3 minutes longer or until pineapple is hot. Serve over hot cooked rice.

1 SERVING: Calories 180; Total Fat 2g (Saturated Fat 0g; Trans Fat 0g); Cholesterol 160mg; Sodium 650mg; Total Carbohydrate 25g (Dietary Fiber 3g); Protein 18g **EXCHANGES:** 1½ Other Carbohydrate, 2½ Very Lean Meat **CARBOHYDRATE CHOICES:** 1½

good eats for kids *This slightly sweet dish is perfect family fare. Kids will enjoy the flavor and it's really easy to eat. High protein and low fat make this a great choice for dinner.*

chili shrimp with honey salsa

prep time: **30 minutes** ▪ start to finish: **30 minutes** ▪ **4 servings**

¾ cup chunky-style salsa

1 tablespoon honey

½ teaspoon ground cumin

1 teaspoon chili powder

1½ lb uncooked deveined peeled large shrimp, tail shells removed if desired

1 tablespoon butter, melted

½ teaspoon seasoned salt

1 Heat gas or charcoal grill. To make foil tray for shrimp, cut 18×12-inch sheet of heavy-duty (or nonstick) foil. Fold up sides and corners to create pan with sides. If using heavy-duty foil, spray foil with cooking spray.

2 In small bowl, mix salsa, honey, cumin and ½ teaspoon of the chili powder; set aside. In foil tray, toss shrimp with butter, remaining ½ teaspoon chili powder and the seasoned salt.

3 Place foil tray with shrimp on grill. Cover grill; cook over medium heat 8 to 10 minutes, stirring shrimp or shaking tray occasionally to turn shrimp, until shrimp are pink. Serve shrimp with salsa mixture.

1 SERVING: Calories 180; Total Fat 4.5g (Saturated Fat 2g; Trans Fat 0g); Cholesterol 250mg; Sodium 820mg; Total Carbohydrate 9g (Dietary Fiber 0g); Protein 26g **EXCHANGES:** ½ Other Carbohydrate, 3½ Very Lean Meat, ½ Fat **CARBOHYDRATE CHOICES:** ½

substitution idea *Shrimp are easy for kids to eat, but scallops are also nice to use for this recipe. Everyone will enjoy the spicy sweet salsa sauce.*

sweet-and-sour pork chops

prep time: **25 minutes** ▪ start to finish: **25 minutes** ▪ **4 servings**

½ cup sweet-and-sour sauce

2 tablespoons chili sauce

¼ teaspoon ground ginger

4 boneless pork loin chops
(about ¾ inch thick)

½ teaspoon garlic powder

½ teaspoon paprika

1 Heat gas or charcoal grill. In 1-quart saucepan, mix sweet-and-sour sauce, chili sauce and ginger. Sprinkle pork chops with garlic powder and paprika.

2 Place pork chops on grill. Cover grill; cook over medium heat 8 to 10 minutes, turning once or twice and brushing with sauce mixture during last 5 minutes of cooking, until pork is no longer pink and meat thermometer inserted in center reads 160°F.

3 Heat any remaining sauce mixture to boiling; serve with pork chops.

1 SERVING: Calories 270; Total Fat 11g (Saturated Fat 4g; Trans Fat 0g); Cholesterol 85mg; Sodium 280mg; Total Carbohydrate 10g (Dietary Fiber 0g); Protein 31g EXCHANGES: ½ Other Carbohydrate, 4½ Lean Meat CARBOHYDRATE CHOICES: ½

good eats for kids   *Lean boneless pork chops are a great source of protein and many important vitamins. They're ideal for kids because you don't need to worry about bones or a lot of fat content. And, because they're a tender cut, kids usually enjoy them.*

pork fajita wraps

prep time: **15 minutes** ▪ start to finish: **30 minutes** ▪ **4 wraps**

¼ cup lime juice

1½ teaspoons ground cumin

¾ teaspoon salt

4 cloves garlic, finely chopped

½ lb pork tenderloin, cut into very thin slices

1 large onion, thinly sliced

3 medium bell peppers, thinly sliced

4 flour tortillas (8 inch)

1 In shallow glass or plastic dish, mix lime juice, cumin, salt and garlic. Stir in pork. Cover and refrigerate, stirring occasionally, at least 15 minutes but no longer than 24 hours.

2 Remove pork from marinade; reserve marinade. Heat 12-inch nonstick skillet over medium-high heat. Cook pork in skillet 3 minutes, stirring once. Stir in onion, bell peppers and marinade. Cook 5 to 8 minutes, stirring frequently, until onion and peppers are crisp-tender.

3 Place ¼ of the pork mixture on center of each tortilla. Fold one end of tortilla up about 1 inch over pork mixture; fold right and left sides over folded end, overlapping.

1 WRAP: Calories 260; Total Fat 6g (Saturated Fat 1.5g; Trans Fat 0g); Cholesterol 35mg; Sodium 680mg; Total Carbohydrate 35g (Dietary Fiber 3g); Protein 18g **EXCHANGES:** 2½ Starch, 1½ Lean Meat **CARBOHYDRATE CHOICES:** 2

good eats for kids *One bell pepper packs a real nutritional punch. It contains 1½ times the vitamin C your body needs daily. You can serve these flavorful fajitas with ½ cup reduced-fat sour cream or plain yogurt and ½ cup salsa stirred together.*

spicy texas chili

prep time: **30 minutes** • start to finish: **30 minutes** • **4 servings** (1½ cups each)

1 lb boneless beef top round steak, cut into ½-inch pieces

½ cup chopped onion (1 medium)

1 medium jalapeño chile, seeded, minced

3 cloves garlic, minced

3 cans (14.5 oz each) diced tomatoes, undrained

4 teaspoons chili powder

¼ teaspoon ground red pepper (cayenne)

Salt, if desired

1 Heat nonstick Dutch oven or 12-inch skillet over medium-high heat. Add beef, onion, chile and garlic; cook about 5 minutes, stirring occasionally, until beef is no longer pink.

2 Stir in all remaining ingredients. Heat to boiling. Reduce heat to medium-low; simmer uncovered 15 to 20 minutes, stirring occasionally, until chili is slightly thickened and flavors are blended. Season to taste with salt.

1 SERVING: Calories 220; Total Fat 4.5g (Saturated Fat 1.5g, Trans Fat 0g); Cholesterol 60mg; Sodium 500mg; Total Carbohydrate 17g (Dietary Fiber 4g); Protein 27g EXCHANGES: 3 Vegetable, 3 Very Lean Meat, ½ Fat CARBOHYDRATE CHOICES: 1

beef stew

prep time: **30 minutes** ▪ start to finish: **30 minutes** ▪ **6 servings** (1¼ cups each)

¾ lb boneless beef top sirloin steak, cut into ½-inch pieces

1 small onion, chopped (⅓ cup)

3 cups frozen southern-style hash-brown potatoes (from 32-oz bag)

1½ cups thinly sliced carrots (1½ medium)

1 cup thinly sliced celery (1¾ medium stalks)

1 jar (4.5 oz) sliced mushrooms, drained

1 envelope (1.5 oz) beef-mushroom soup mix (dry)

¼ teaspoon dried thyme leaves, crushed

¼ teaspoon salt, if desired

⅛ teaspoon pepper

3 cups water

Chopped fresh parsley, if desired

1 Heat nonstick Dutch oven or 4-quart saucepan over medium-high heat. Add beef and onion; cook 5 minutes, stirring occasionally, until beef is browned.

2 Stir in potatoes, carrots, celery and mushrooms. Cook 2 minutes, stirring frequently. Stir in remaining ingredients. Heat to boiling. Reduce heat to low; simmer uncovered about 15 minutes or until vegetables are tender. Sprinkle individual servings with chopped fresh parsley.

1 SERVING: Calories 180; Total Fat 2.5g (Saturated Fat 1g; Trans Fat 0g); Cholesterol 40mg; Sodium 770mg; Total Carbohydrate 21g (Dietary Fiber 3g); Protein 18g **EXCHANGES:** 1 Starch, 1 Vegetable, 2 Very Lean Meat **CARBOHYDRATE CHOICES:** 1½

good eats for kids   *This hearty stew is an excellent source of vitamin A and also contributes to the vitamin C and iron needs of both kids and adults.*

super speedy chili

prep time: **15 minutes** • start to finish: **15 minutes** • **4 servings** (1⅓ cups each)

½ lb lean (at least 80%)
  ground beef

2 cans (14.5 oz each)
  reduced-sodium stewed
  tomatoes, undrained,
  cut up

1 can (15 oz) spicy chili
  beans, undrained

3 teaspoons chili powder

Shredded Cheddar cheese,
  if desired

1 In 3-quart saucepan or 10-inch skillet, cook beef over medium-high heat, stirring frequently, until thoroughly cooked; drain.

2 Stir in tomatoes, chili beans and chili powder. Heat to boiling. Reduce heat to medium-low; simmer uncovered 5 minutes, stirring occasionally. Top individual servings with cheese.

1 SERVING: Calories 250; Total Fat 8g (Saturated Fat 2.5g; Trans Fat 0g); Cholesterol 35mg; Sodium 840mg; Total Carbohydrate 27g (Dietary Fiber 7g); Protein 17g **EXCHANGES:** 1 Starch, 2 Vegetable, 1½ Medium-Fat Meat **CARBOHYDRATE CHOICES:** 2

good eats for kids *Although this chili is already fairly low in fat, you could substitute lean ground turkey for the ground beef and reduce the fat even further.*

chipotle chicken pizza

prep time: **15 minutes** • start to finish: **25 minutes** • **8 servings**

1 can (11 oz) refrigerated thin pizza crust

1 cup chunky-style mild salsa

½ to 1 chipotle chile in adobo sauce, finely chopped (from 7-oz can)

1 package (5 oz) refrigerated cooked southwestern-style chicken breast strips

¼ cup chopped onion

½ cup chopped red bell pepper

½ cup chopped green bell pepper

1½ cups shredded reduced-fat Mexican cheese blend (6 oz)

1 Heat oven to 400°F. Spray or grease 15×10×1-inch or larger dark or nonstick cookie sheet. Unroll dough on cookie sheet; starting at center, press dough into 15×10-inch rectangle.

2 In small bowl, mix salsa and chipotle chile; spread to within ½ inch of edges of dough.

3 Top with chicken strips, onion and peppers; sprinkle with cheese.

4 Bake 10 to 12 minutes or until crust is golden brown and cheese is melted. Cut into 8 servings.

1 SERVING: Calories 210; Total Fat 7g (Saturated Fat 3g; Trans Fat 0g); Cholesterol 20mg; Sodium 690mg; Total Carbohydrate 23g (Dietary Fiber 1g); Protein 13g **EXCHANGES:** 1½ Starch, 1 Lean Meat, ½ Fat **CARBOHYDRATE CHOICES:** 1½

DOUGHBOY TIPS

Teach the kids a great kitchen lesson by showing them how to press the dough onto the cookie sheet— and let them help.

substitution idea *Kick up the heat and use hot salsa instead of the mild.*

mexican pasta skillet

prep time: **30 minutes** ▪ start to finish: **30 minutes** ▪ **6 servings** (1⅓ cups each)

1 lb extra-lean (at least 90%) ground beef

1 jar (16 oz) mild chunky-style salsa

1 can (8 oz) tomato sauce

1½ cups water

2 cups uncooked regular or multigrain elbow macaroni

1 cup frozen corn

½ cup shredded reduced-fat sharp Cheddar cheese (2 oz)

1 In 12-inch skillet, cook beef over medium-high heat 5 to 7 minutes, stirring occasionally, until thoroughly cooked; drain.

2 Stir in salsa, tomato sauce and water. Heat to boiling. Stir in macaroni and corn. Reduce heat; cover and simmer 12 to 15 minutes, stirring occasionally, until macaroni is tender.

3 Sprinkle with cheese. Cover; let stand 1 to 2 minutes or until cheese is melted.

1 SERVING: Calories 370; Total Fat 6g (Saturated Fat 2.5g; Trans Fat 0g); Cholesterol 45mg; Sodium 650mg; Total Carbohydrate 53g (Dietary Fiber 3g); Protein 25g **EXCHANGES:** 3½ Starch, 2 Lean Meat **CARBOHYDRATE CHOICES:** 3½

DOUGHBOY TIPS

Let the kids toss a crisp green salad with their favorite low-fat dressing and then serve it with this family-style skillet meal.

substitution idea *It's easy to substitute lean ground turkey for the ground beef, if you like. And, if your family likes things a little spicier, go bold with medium salsa instead of the mild.*

cheesy vegetable risotto

prep time: **30 minutes** · start to finish: **30 minutes** · **8 servings** (½ cup each)

1 tablespoon butter or margarine

2 tablespoons olive or vegetable oil

1 large onion, chopped (1 cup)

1 clove garlic, finely chopped

1 cup uncooked Arborio rice

1 carton (32 oz) reduced-sodium chicken broth (4 cups), warmed

1 bag (12 oz) frozen broccoli, carrots and cauliflower in a cheese flavored sauce

½ cup shredded Parmesan cheese

2 tablespoons chopped fresh parsley

¼ teaspoon coarse ground pepper

1 In 10-inch nonstick skillet, heat butter and oil over medium-high heat until butter is melted. Add onion and garlic; cook 3 to 4 minutes, stirring frequently, until onion is tender.

2 Stir in rice. Cook, stirring occasionally, until edges of kernels are translucent. Stir in ½ cup of the broth. Cook 2 to 3 minutes, stirring constantly, until broth is absorbed.

3 Reduce heat to medium. Stir in 1½ cups of the broth; cook uncovered about 5 minutes, stirring frequently, until broth is absorbed. Stir in another 1 cup of the broth; cook uncovered about 5 minutes longer, stirring frequently, until broth is absorbed.

4 Stir in remaining 1 cup broth. Cook about 8 minutes, stirring frequently, until rice is tender and mixture is creamy. Meanwhile, cook frozen vegetables as directed on bag. Stir vegetables, Parmesan cheese, parsley and pepper into rice mixture.

1 SERVING: Calories 200; Total Fat 7g (Saturated Fat 2.5g; Trans Fat 0g); Cholesterol 10mg; Sodium 840mg; Total Carbohydrate 26g (Dietary Fiber 1g); Protein 7g **EXCHANGES:** 1½ Starch, 1 Vegetable, 1 Fat CARBOHYDRATE CHOICES: 2

good eats for kids *We love the way the veggies are part of this easy dish. Kids will hardly notice they are included because they're covered in the cheesy rich mixture.*

margherita pizza

prep time: **15 minutes** ▪ start to finish: **30 minutes** ▪ **8 servings**

Cornmeal, if desired

1 can (13.8 oz) refrigerated classic pizza crust or 1 can (11 oz) refrigerated thin pizza crust

2 teaspoons olive oil

1 teaspoon finely chopped garlic

1½ cups shredded mozzarella cheese (6 oz)

¼ cup shredded fresh Parmesan cheese

20 (¼-inch-thick) slices plum (Roma) tomatoes (about 6 medium)

⅓ cup thin fresh basil strips

1 If using classic crust: Heat oven to 425°F. If using thin crust: Heat oven to 400°F.

2 Spray or grease 15×10×1-inch or larger dark or nonstick cookie sheet. Sprinkle cookie sheet with cornmeal. Unroll dough on cookie sheet. Starting at center, press out dough into 15×10-inch rectangle. Brush dough with oil; sprinkle evenly with garlic.

3 Sprinkle mozzarella and Parmesan cheeses over crust. Arrange tomato slices over cheese. Sprinkle with half of the basil.

4 Bake classic crust 14 to 16 minutes, thin crust 12 to 14 minutes, or until crust is deep golden brown. Sprinkle remaining half of basil over pizza. Cut into 8 servings.

1 SERVING: Calories 220; Total Fat 8g (Saturated Fat 4g; Trans Fat 0g); Cholesterol 15mg; Sodium 520mg; Total Carbohydrate 26g (Dietary Fiber 1g); Protein 11g EXCHANGES: 1½ Starch, ½ Vegetable, ½ Medium-Fat Meat, 1 Fat CARBOHYDRATE CHOICES: 2

substitution idea *Simple ingredients top this easy pizza. The fresh basil is really nice, but about 1 teaspoon dried can be substituted if you don't have it on hand. Also, an Italian cheese blend can be used instead of the mozzarella and Parmesan cheeses.*

make it a pizza-perfect night

We know that kids like pizza, so why not have a pizza night at your house? Using refrigerated pizza dough makes it super easy. Just roll or press out the dough, top and bake. One of our favorites is the Family Cheese Pizza on page 120. You can be as creative as you like with extra toppings. With young children, it's fun to create a face or other design with toppings that could include any of these ideas.

- Chopped tomatoes
- Sliced olives
- Chopped or sliced bell pepper
- Shredded cheese
- Red onion rings or pieces
- Chopped cooked chicken
- Cooked crumbled extra-lean ground beef
- Cooked lean turkey Italian sausage
- Small pineapple wedges

super FAST

family cheese pizza

prep time: **5 minutes** ▪ start to finish: **20 minutes** ▪ **6 servings**

Cornmeal, if desired

1 can (13.8 oz) refrigerated classic pizza crust or 1 can (11 oz) refrigerated thin pizza crust

1 cup pizza sauce

1 cup shredded mozzarella cheese (4 oz)

1 If using classic crust: Heat oven to 425°F. Spray or grease cookie sheet. Sprinkle cornmeal on cookie sheet. Unroll dough and place on cookie sheet; starting at center, press out dough to edge of cookie sheet. If using thin crust: Heat oven to 400°F. Spray or grease 15×10×1-inch or larger dark or nonstick cookie sheet. Sprinkle cornmeal on cookie sheet. Unroll dough on cookie sheet. Starting at center, press dough into 15×10-inch rectangle.*

2 Spread pizza sauce over dough to within ½ inch of edge. Top with mozzarella cheese.

3 Bake classic crust 10 to 15 minutes, thin crust 8 to 13 minutes, or until crust is golden brown. Cut into 6 servings.

1 SERVING: Calories 240; Total Fat 6g (Saturated Fat 3g; Trans Fat 0g); Cholesterol 10mg; Sodium 650mg; Total Carbohydrate 35g (Dietary Fiber 2g); Protein 10g EXCHANGES: 2 Starch, ½ Other Carbohydrate, ½ High-Fat Meat CARBOHYDRATE CHOICES: 2

To make dough strips in photo on page 119, before pressing out dough, cut ¼ inch strips of dough from short side of dough and ¼ inch strips of dough from long side. After pressing out dough, place strips on top of dough, pressing lightly. Top as desired.

substitution idea   *Change up the cheese flavor as you like when you make this easy pizza. Most kids like the mild flavor of mozzarella, but a mix of Italian cheeses would also be good. If your kids love the flavor of pepperoni, add some turkey pepperoni to the pizza before putting it in the oven—as we did in the photo to the right.*

canadian bacon and pineapple pizza

prep time: **30 minutes** ▪ start to finish: **30 minutes** ▪ 8 servings

1 can (13.8 oz) refrigerated classic pizza crust or 1 can (11 oz) refrigerated thin pizza crust

1 package (6 oz) sliced provolone cheese

1 package (5 to 6 oz) sliced Canadian bacon

1 can (8 oz) pineapple chunks in unsweetened juice, well drained on paper towels

½ cup thinly sliced red onion

½ cup chopped green bell pepper

½ cup shredded Cheddar cheese (2 oz)

1 If using classic crust: Heat oven to 425°F. Spray or grease 12-inch pizza pan or 13 ×9-inch pan. Unroll dough in pan. Starting at center, press dough to edge of pan. If using thin crust: Heat oven to 400°F. Spray or grease 15×10×1-inch or larger dark or nonstick cookie sheet. Unroll dough on cookie sheet; starting at center, press out dough into 15×10-inch rectangle.

2 Top dough with provolone cheese, cutting to fit. Arrange Canadian bacon, pineapple, onion and bell pepper over provolone cheese to within ½ inch of edges. Sprinkle with Cheddar cheese.

3 Bake classic crust 16 to 20 minutes, thin crust 10 to 14 minutes, or until crust is deep golden brown. Cut into 8 servings.

1 SERVING: Calories 270; Total Fat 11g (Saturated Fat 6g; Trans Fat 0g); Cholesterol 30mg; Sodium 810mg; Total Carbohydrate 30g (Dietary Fiber 0g); Protein 14g EXCHANGES: 1 Starch, 1 Other Carbohydrate, 1½ Medium-Fat Meat, ½ Fat CARBOHYDRATE CHOICES: 2

substitution idea *Canadian Bacon is a great choice for this pizza, but if you have some lean ham, it will be good too. Also, mozzarella cheese can be used instead of the Cheddar if your family prefers it.*

Broccoli and Tomatoes, see page 140

CHAPTER FOUR

sides

lettuce bundles

prep time: **30 minutes** ▪ start to finish: **30 minutes** ▪ **8 servings** (3 bundles and 1 tablespoon sauce each)

½ cup orange juice

2 tablespoons sugar

1 teaspoon cornstarch

⅛ teaspoon crushed red pepper flakes

1 tablespoon cider vinegar

½ teaspoon grated orange peel

2 heads butterhead (Boston or Bibb) lettuce, separated into 24 medium leaves (or 12 large leaves, cut in half)

1 large red bell pepper, cut into thin 2-inch-long strips (about 1½ cups)

½ English cucumber, cut into julienne (matchstick-cut) strips (1 cup)

1 cup julienne (matchstick-cut) carrots

1 In 2-quart saucepan, mix orange juice, sugar, cornstarch and pepper flakes with whisk until cornstarch is completely dissolved. Heat to boiling over medium-high heat, stirring frequently. Boil 1 minute, stirring frequently. Remove from heat; stir in vinegar and orange peel. Cool completely, about 15 minutes.

2 Meanwhile, on center of each lettuce leaf, place equal amounts of bell pepper, cucumber and carrots; roll up, leaving ends open. Secure with toothpick; place on serving platter. Serve bundles with sauce.

1 SERVING: Calories 40; Total Fat 0g (Saturated Fat 0g; Trans Fat 0g); Cholesterol 0mg; Sodium 15mg; Total Carbohydrate 9g (Dietary Fiber 1g); Protein 1g EXCHANGES: 1½ Vegetable CARBOHYDRATE CHOICES: ½

 **DOUGHBOY TIPS**

These are great fun to make and eat, and kids can help. Cut the remaining half of the cucumber into ¼-inch-thick slices and place on a serving plate to be used as additional dippers for the sauce.

honey-mustard coleslaw with apples

prep time: **15 minutes** ▪ start to finish: **15 minutes** ▪ **12 servings** (¾ cup each)

1 bag (16 oz) coleslaw mix (8 cups)

½ cup chopped green onions (8 medium)

2 medium apples, cored and cut into julienne (matchstick) pieces

1 cup reduced-fat honey-mustard dressing

1 In large bowl, toss all ingredients.

2 Serve immediately, or cover and refrigerate up to 24 hours before serving.

1 SERVING: Calories 80; Total Fat 2.5g (Saturated Fat 0g; Trans Fat 0g); Cholesterol 0mg; Sodium 210mg; Total Carbohydrate 12g (Dietary Fiber 2g); Protein 0g **EXCHANGES:** ½ Other Carbohydrate, 1 Vegetable, ½ Fat **CARBOHYDRATE CHOICES:** 1

substitution idea   *Instead of using a bag of coleslaw mix, toss 7 cups of shredded green and red cabbage with 1 cup shredded carrots.*

super FAST | orange-carrot slaw

prep time: **15 minutes** ▪ start to finish: **15 minutes** ▪ **8 servings** (½ cup each)

SALAD

3 cups shredded carrots

1 can (11 oz) mandarin orange segments, drained

1 cup halved seedless green grapes

DRESSING

½ cup orange low-fat yogurt

1 teaspoon cider vinegar

¼ teaspoon ground ginger

1 In serving bowl, mix salad ingredients.

2 In small bowl, mix dressing ingredients. Pour dressing over salad; mix thoroughly. Serve immediately, or cover and refrigerate until serving time.

1 SERVING: Calories 60; Total Fat 0g (Saturated Fat 0g; Trans Fat 0g); Cholesterol 0mg; Sodium 40mg; Total Carbohydrate 13g (Dietary Fiber 1g); Protein 1g **EXCHANGES:** ½ Fruit, ½ Vegetable **CARBOHYDRATE CHOICES:** 1

DOUGHBOY TIPS

Here's a great salad for kids to help make. If you purchase the carrots shredded or shred them ahead of time, all they have to do is mix everything together.

salad bar savvy for dinner

When you're looking for a great idea to serve with your evening meal, why not try a salad bar? It's a creative way to offer a variety of healthy choices that are interesting and tasty too. Everyone can choose what they like, and you know they're getting the nutrition they need. Here are some great ideas to get you started—and remember that mixing and matching makes it fun!

- Leaf lettuce
- Romaine lettuce
- Bibb lettuce
- Baby spinach leaves
- Shredded red or green cabbage
- Grape, cherry or sliced tomatoes

- Cubed cucumber
- Avocado slices
- Shredded carrots
- Small broccoli or cauliflower florets

- Cooked shelled edamame
- Cooked corn
- Sliced olives

super FAST | fresh pear salad

prep time: **15 minutes** • start to finish: **15 minutes** • **6 servings**

DRESSING

3 tablespoons cider vinegar

3 tablespoons raspberry jam

1 tablespoon vegetable oil

SALAD

3 cups torn escarole
 or leaf lettuce

2 small pears, cored

1 tablespoon chopped
 hazelnuts (filberts)

1 In small jar with tight-fitting lid, shake dressing ingredients. Set aside.

2 Arrange escarole on 6 salad plates. Thinly slice pears; arrange slices over lettuce. Sprinkle hazelnuts over salads; drizzle with dressing. Serve immediately.

1 SERVING: Calories 90; Total Fat 3g (Saturated Fat 0g; Trans Fat 0g); Cholesterol 0mg; Sodium 5mg; Total Carbohydrate 15g (Dietary Fiber 2g); Protein 0g **EXCHANGES:** 1 Other Carbohydrate, ½ Fat **CARBOHYDRATE CHOICES:** 1

substitution idea   *The hazelnuts add a nice crunch to this salad, but you can omit them if you like. Romaine is a good option instead of the escarole or leaf lettuce.*

confetti pasta salad

prep time: **25 minutes** ▪ start to finish: **25 minutes** ▪ **8 servings**

8 oz uncooked bow-tie (farfalle) pasta

2 cups frozen mixed vegetables

¼ cup coarsely chopped red onion

1 medium tomato, chopped

½ cup reduced-fat Italian dressing

1 Cook pasta as directed on package, adding frozen mixed vegetables during last 5 to 7 minutes of cooking time; cook until vegetables are tender. Drain; rinse with cold water. Drain well.

2 In medium bowl, gently toss cooled cooked pasta and vegetables, and remaining ingredients to coat. Serve immediately or cover and refrigerate until serving time.

1 SERVING: Calories 150; Total Fat 3.5g (Saturated Fat 0.5g; Trans Fat 0g); Cholesterol 0mg; Sodium 200mg; Total Carbohydrate 25g (Dietary Fiber 2g); Protein 4g EXCHANGES: 1½ Starch, ½ Vegetable, ½ Fat CARBOHYDRATE CHOICES: 1½

good eats for kids *Here's a great way to serve nutrition-rich veggies to the kids. You can choose to use the mixed veggies or use another vegetable instead if your kids prefer something else.*

herb vegetable couscous

prep time: **15 minutes** ▪ start to finish: **15 minutes** ▪ **6 servings** (½ cup each)

1 cup chicken broth

⅔ cup frozen peas

⅛ teaspoon salt

⅛ teaspoon pepper

1 teaspoon chopped fresh thyme or ¼ teaspoon dried thyme leaves

1 garlic clove, minced

¾ cup uncooked couscous

1 medium tomato, seeded, chopped

1 In medium saucepan, combine broth, peas, salt, pepper, thyme and garlic. Bring to a boil.

2 Remove saucepan from heat; stir in couscous and tomato. Cover; let stand 5 minutes. Fluff with fork before serving.

1 SERVING: Calories 100; Total Fat 0g (Saturated Fat 0g, Trans Fat 0g); Cholesterol 0mg; Sodium 230mg; Total Carbohydrate 20g (Dietary Fiber 2g); Protein 4g   EXCHANGES: 1 Starch, ½ Vegetable   CARBOHYDRATE CHOICES: 1

super FAST | # baby peas with lemon-pepper and honey

prep time: **15 minutes** ▪ start to finish: **15 minutes** ▪ **5 servings** (⅔ cup each)

2 bags (12 oz each) frozen baby sweet peas

2 teaspoons honey

1 teaspoon margarine or butter

¼ teaspoon lemon-pepper seasoning

¼ teaspoon salt

¼ to ½ teaspoon grated lemon peel

1 Cook peas as directed on bag; drain.

2 Place in medium bowl. Add honey, margarine, lemon-pepper seasoning and salt; toss to coat. Sprinkle with lemon peel.

1 SERVING: Calories 110; Total Fat 1g (Saturated Fat 0.5g, Trans Fat 0g); Cholesterol 0mg; Sodium 230mg; Total Carbohydrate 19g (Dietary Fiber 4g); Protein 6g **EXCHANGES:** ½ Other Carbohydrate, 2 Vegetable **CARBOHYDRATE CHOICES:** 1

super FAST | black beans in boo bowls

prep time: **15 minutes** ▪ start to finish: **15 minutes** ▪ **6 servings** (½ cup each)

3 large oranges

2 cans (15 oz each) black beans, drained, rinsed

½ cup chunky-style salsa

⅓ cup shredded mild Cheddar cheese

1 Using small paring knife, make zigzag cut around center of each orange, cutting orange in half; pull halves apart. Using grapefruit spoon or small paring knife, remove orange segments; place in resealable food-storage plastic bag, and save for another use.

2 In 1-quart saucepan, heat beans and salsa over medium-high heat, stirring constantly, until hot. Spoon bean mixture into orange shells.

3 Spoon about 1 tablespoon cheese on top of each. Place on microwavable plate; microwave on High 1 to 2 minutes or until cheese starts to melt.

1 SERVING: Calories 200; Total Fat 3g (Saturated Fat 1.5g; Trans Fat 0g); Cholesterol 5mg; Sodium 190mg; Total Carbohydrate 33g (Dietary Fiber 12g); Protein 11g **EXCHANGES:** 1½ Starch, ½ Other Carbohydrate, 1 Lean Meat **CARBOHYDRATE CHOICES:** 2

DOUGHBOY TIPS

Kids will be intrigued with these tasty filled orange halves. Serve them for Halloween or any time you're in the mood for something fun. You can save the orange segments to serve for lunch the next day.

super FAST | broccoli and tomatoes

prep time: **10 minutes** • start to finish: **10 minutes** • **6 servings** (¾ cup each)

½ cup water

4 cups bite-sized pieces fresh broccoli

1 pint (2 cups) cherry tomatoes, halved

½ teaspoon dried dill weed

¼ teaspoon lemon-pepper seasoning

1 In 4-quart saucepan, heat water to boiling. Add broccoli; return to boiling.

2 Reduce heat; simmer over medium-low heat 4 to 6 minutes or until broccoli is crisp-tender. Add tomatoes; cook 1 minute. Drain; toss with dill and lemon-pepper seasoning.

1 SERVING: Calories 40; Total Fat 0g (Saturated Fat 0g; Trans Fat 0g); Cholesterol 0mg; Sodium 35mg; Total Carbohydrate 6g (Dietary Fiber 2g); Protein 2g **EXCHANGES:** 1 Vegetable **CARBOHYDRATE CHOICES:** ½

good eats for kids   *Mixing the broccoli with tomatoes is a clever way to serve two really great-for-you foods at one time to kids of all ages.*

substitution idea   *One bag (1 pound) of frozen cut broccoli can be substituted for the fresh broccoli. Prepare it as directed on the bag.*

See photo on page 124.

super FAST | lemon-garlic broccoli

prep time: **15 minutes** • start to finish: **15 minutes** • **6 servings** (½ cup each)

2 bags (12 oz each) frozen broccoli florets

2 teaspoons olive or canola oil

6 cloves garlic, finely chopped

1 tablespoon grated lemon peel

½ teaspoon salt

⅛ teaspoon pepper

1 Cook broccoli as directed on bag; set aside.

2 In 10-inch skillet, heat oil over medium heat. Cook garlic in oil about 1 minute, stirring frequently, until golden brown.

3 Stir in broccoli; cook 1 minute. Stir in lemon peel, salt and pepper.

1 SERVING: Calories 50; Total Fat 1.5g (Saturated Fat 0g; Trans Fat 0g); Cholesterol 0mg; Sodium 210mg; Total Carbohydrate 7g (Dietary Fiber 3g); Protein 3g **EXCHANGES:** 1 Vegetable, ½ Fat **CARBOHYDRATE CHOICES:** ½

substitution idea *This flavorful broccoli dish could easily become a family favorite. Change the taste just a bit by using orange or lime peel instead of the lemon.*

honey-mustard glazed carrots

prep time: **20 minutes** • start to finish: **20 minutes** • **6 servings** (½ cup each)

1 bag (1 lb) ready-to-eat baby-cut carrots

2 tablespoons honey

1 tablespoon olive or canola oil

2 teaspoons Dijon mustard

1 tablespoon fresh chopped parsley

¼ teaspoon salt

⅛ teaspoon pepper

1 In 2-quart saucepan, heat ½ cup water to boiling. Add carrots. Cover; simmer 10 to 15 minutes or until tender. Drain.

2 In medium bowl, mix remaining ingredients. Add carrots; toss lightly to coat.

1 SERVING: Calories 80; Total Fat 2.5g (Saturated Fat 0g; Trans Fat 0g); Cholesterol 0mg; Sodium 190mg; Total Carbohydrate 13g (Dietary Fiber 2g); Protein 0g **EXCHANGES:** ½ Other Carbohydrate, 1 Vegetable, ½ Fat **CARBOHYDRATE CHOICES:** 1

good eats for kids   *Carrots provide a healthy dose of vitamin A, and kids usually like them. They're especially good with the sweet sauce in this recipe. Plus, baby carrots are really easy to fix because they don't need to be peeled.*

dilly buttered carrots and rotini

prep time: **10 minutes** ▪ start to finish: **20 minutes** ▪ **8 servings** (½ cup each)

1 cup uncooked rainbow or plain rotini pasta (3 oz)

2 cups ready-to-eat baby-cut carrots, cut in half lengthwise and crosswise

1 tablespoon butter

1 teaspoon chopped fresh or ¼ teaspoon dried dill weed

¼ teaspoon salt

Dash pepper

1 In 3-quart saucepan, cook pasta as directed on package, adding carrots during last 2 to 3 minutes of cooking time; cook until pasta is tender and carrots are crisp-tender. Drain; return to saucepan.

2 Add butter, dill, salt and pepper; toss gently to coat.

1 SERVING: Calories 80; Total Fat 2g (Saturated Fat 1g; Trans Fat 0g); Cholesterol 0mg; Sodium 160mg; Total Carbohydrate 14g (Dietary Fiber 2g); Protein 2g **EXCHANGES:** 1 Starch **CARBOHYDRATE CHOICES:** 1

good eats for kids *This recipe calls for regular rotini but it might be a great opportunity to introduce one of the new whole grain pasta products into the menu.*

skillet acorn squash

prep time: **25 minutes** ▪ start to finish: **25 minutes** ▪ **4 servings**

1 large acorn squash (2 lb)

½ cup apple juice

1 tablespoon margarine
or butter

¼ teaspoon ground
cinnamon

1 Trim ends off squash. Stand squash on end; cut in half. Remove and discard seeds and fiber. Cut each squash half crosswise into ½-inch-thick slices.

2 In 12-inch nonstick skillet, mix apple juice, margarine and cinnamon. Add squash. Heat to boiling. Reduce heat; cover and simmer 10 minutes.

3 Turn slices; cover and simmer 5 to 8 minutes longer or until squash is tender.

1 SERVING: Calories 140; Total Fat 3g (Saturated Fat 0.5g; Trans Fat 0.5g); Cholesterol 0mg; Sodium 30mg; Total Carbohydrate 27g (Dietary Fiber 7g); Protein 1g **EXCHANGES:** 1 Starch, ½ Other Carbohydrate, ½ Fat **CARBOHYDRATE CHOICES:** 2

good eats for kids *This recipe calls for acorn squash, but you could use buttercup squash instead. They're both great sources of vitamin A and are high in fiber and low in fat.*

roasted seasoned cauliflower

prep time: **10 minutes** ▪ start to finish: **30 minutes** ▪ **8 servings** (½ cup each)

1 head cauliflower (1½ lb), divided into large florets (about 6 cups)

4 teaspoons olive or canola oil

1 teaspoon chili powder

1 teaspoon garlic powder

⅛ teaspoon salt

1 Heat oven to 400°F. Line 15×10×1-inch pan with foil; spray with cooking spray.

2 Cut cauliflower florets into ½-inch slices; place in 3-quart bowl.

3 In small bowl, mix remaining ingredients. Pour over cauliflower; toss to coat. Spread in pan.

4 Roast uncovered 20 to 25 minutes, turning after 10 minutes or until cauliflower is tender and slightly brown around edges.

1 SERVING: Calories 35; Total Fat 2.5g (Saturated Fat 0g; Trans Fat 0g); Cholesterol 0mg; Sodium 55mg; Total Carbohydrate 3g (Dietary Fiber 1g); Protein 1g **EXCHANGES:** ½ Vegetable, ½ Fat **CARBOHYDRATE CHOICES:** 0

DOUGHBOY TIPS

Roasting the cauliflower gives it a slightly sweet flavor—ideal for introducing this veggie to kids. Be sure to toss the cauliflower with the oil mixture in a bowl instead of in the pan to be sure that it's evenly coated with the spices.

corn and sweet bean sauté

prep time: **30 minutes** ▪ start to finish: **30 minutes** ▪ **6 servings** (½ cup each)

1 bag (12 oz) frozen whole kernel corn

1 teaspoon butter or margarine

2 teaspoons canola oil

1 small onion, finely chopped (¼ cup)

1½ cups frozen shelled edamame (green soybeans)

½ cup reduced-sodium chicken broth (from 32-oz carton)

¼ teaspoon salt

¼ cup slivered fresh basil leaves

1 In 2-quart saucepan, heat 2 inches of water to boiling. Add corn; reduce heat. Simmer uncovered 5 minutes; drain. Rinse with cold water; drain and set aside.

2 In 10-inch skillet, heat butter and oil over medium-high heat until butter is melted. Add onion; cook 2 to 3 minutes, stirring frequently, until crisp-tender.

3 Stir in edamame and broth. Heat to boiling; reduce heat. Simmer uncovered about 10 minutes, stirring occasionally, until edamame are tender.

4 Stir in corn and salt. Cook 4 to 6 minutes, stirring occasionally, until corn is hot. Sprinkle with basil just before serving.

1 SERVING: Calories 130; Total Fat 4.5g (Saturated Fat 1g; Trans Fat 0g); Cholesterol 0mg; Sodium 150mg; Total Carbohydrate 15g (Dietary Fiber 3g); Protein 6g EXCHANGES: 1 Starch, 1 Fat CARBOHYDRATE CHOICES: 1

good eats for kids *Mild-flavored green soybeans, or edamame, are a good source of heart-healthy soy protein. They're slightly sweet and really easy for kids to eat. You'll find them in the freezer section of most supermarkets.*

spicy asian green beans

prep time: **20 minutes** ▪ start to finish: **20 minutes** ▪ **4 servings** (¾ cup each)

BEANS

1 bag (14 oz) frozen whole green beans

SAUCE

¼ cup orange juice

1 teaspoon cornstarch

3 tablespoons reduced-sodium soy sauce

⅛ to ¼ teaspoon crushed red pepper flakes

1 small clove garlic, finely chopped

1 Cook green beans as directed on bag. Drain; place in serving bowl.

2 Meanwhile, in 1-quart saucepan, mix sauce ingredients until well blended. Heat to boiling. Reduce heat to low; simmer 1 to 2 minutes, stirring constantly, until thickened and clear.

3 Stir sauce into cooked green beans to coat.

1 SERVING: Calories 50; Total Fat 0g (Saturated Fat 0g; Trans Fat 0g); Cholesterol 0mg; Sodium 400mg; Total Carbohydrate 9g (Dietary Fiber 3g); Protein 2g EXCHANGES: ½ Other Carbohydrate, 1 Vegetable CARBOHYDRATE CHOICES: ½

good eats for kids   *Green beans provide fiber and vitamin A. These two nutrients are important for good health.*

maple-glazed sweet potatoes

prep time: **25 minutes** ▪ start to finish: **25 minutes** ▪ **8 servings** (½ cup each)

1 cup apple juice

4 teaspoons cornstarch

½ cup maple-flavored syrup

½ teaspoon ground cinnamon

1 tablespoon margarine or butter

⅛ teaspoon salt

2 lb sweet potatoes (about 3 large), peeled, cut into ¾-inch cubes (about 5 cups)

2 tablespoons chopped pecans

1 In small bowl, mix 2 tablespoons of the apple juice and the cornstarch. Set aside.

2 In 12-inch nonstick skillet or Dutch oven, mix remaining apple juice, the syrup, cinnamon, margarine and salt. Heat to boiling. Add sweet potatoes; stir to coat well. Return to boiling. Reduce heat; cover and simmer 8 to 10 minutes or just until sweet potatoes are tender.

3 Stir cornstarch mixture into sweet potato mixture; cook and stir over medium-high heat until bubbly and thickened. Spoon into serving bowl. Sprinkle with pecans.

1 SERVING: Calories 160; Total Fat 3g (Saturated Fat 0g; Trans Fat 0g); Cholesterol 0mg; Sodium 80mg; Total Carbohydrate 33g (Dietary Fiber 2g); Protein 1g **EXCHANGES:** 1 Starch, 1 Other Carbohydrate, ½ Fat **CARBOHYDRATE CHOICES:** 2

good eats for kids *Kids and adults will enjoy these maple-glazed sweet potatoes that are rich in vitamin A and fiber. You'll find that the bright orange or red varieties are sweeter than the lighter-colored ones.*

Sparkly Popcorn, see page 154

CHAPTER FIVE

snacks and treats

super FAST | sparkly popcorn

prep time: **15 minutes** ■ start to finish: **15 minutes** ■ **16 servings** (½ cup each)

1 snack-size bag (1.75 oz) reduced-fat microwave popcorn, popped

2 cups Trix® cereal

1 tablespoon edible glitter

1 In large bowl, gently mix all ingredients.

2 Store tightly covered.

1 SERVING: Calories 30; Total Fat 0.5g (Saturated Fat 0g; Trans Fat 0g); Cholesterol 0mg; Sodium 55mg; Total Carbohydrate 5g (Dietary Fiber 0g); Protein 0g **EXCHANGES:** ½ Starch **CARBOHYDRATE CHOICES:** ½

DOUGHBOY TIPS

In search of edible glitter? You can find it at craft stores in the cake decorating department or baking specialty stores. If you still have trouble tracking it down, just use your favorite colored sugar instead. What fun for kids to sprinkle the glitter on the popcorn!

See photo on page 152.

hearty multi-grain snack

prep time: **15 minutes** ▪ start to finish: **30 minutes** ▪ **16 servings** (¼ cup each)

1 egg white

¼ teaspoon salt

⅓ cup packed brown sugar

1 teaspoon ground cinnamon

3 cups MultiGrain Cheerios® cereal

⅓ cup coarsely chopped pecans

1 Heat oven to 300°F. Lightly grease cookie sheet.

2 In large bowl, beat egg white using electric mixer on high speed until foamy; beat in salt. Gradually beat in brown sugar until thick and glossy. Gently stir in cinnamon, cereal and pecans until completely coated. Spread as thinly as possible on cookie sheet.

3 Bake 12 to 15 minutes or until set. Immediately remove from cookie sheet to cold cookie sheet or large pan. Cool slightly, or until you can break it into pieces. Store in airtight container.

1 SERVING: Calories 60; Total Fat 2g (Saturated Fat 0g; Trans Fat 0g); Cholesterol 0mg; Sodium 80mg; Total Carbohydrate 9g (Dietary Fiber 1g); Protein 0g EXCHANGES: ½ Other Carbohydrate, ½ Fat CARBOHYDRATE CHOICES: ½

good eats for kids   *Because nuts are high in fat, it's good to keep portions small. But they're really good for all of us, and because the fat in nuts is unsaturated, eating them may help keep our cholesterol lower. This tasty snack can be eaten when slightly cooled, but you can break it into pieces when it's fully cooled.*

whole-grain snack mix

prep time: **5 minutes** ▪ start to finish: **5 minutes** ▪ **28 servings** (¼ cup each)

2 cups Fiber One® original bran cereal

2 cups Fiber One® Honey Clusters® cereal

2 cups Honey Nut Cheerios cereal

1 cup raisins

1 cup peanuts, if desired

1 cup carob chips, if desired

1 In large bowl or gallon-size resealable food-storage plastic bag, mix ingredients.

2 Store tightly covered.

1 SERVING: Calories 60; Total Fat 0g (Saturated Fat 0g; Trans Fat 0g); Cholesterol 0mg; Sodium 55mg; Total Carbohydrate 13g (Dietary Fiber 3g); Protein 1g **EXCHANGES:** 1 Starch **CARBOHYDRATE CHOICES:** 1

good eats for kids   *Look for carob chips in health food, specialty and large grocery stores. Carob comes from a tropical tree and has a chocolate-like flavor and texture. You could use chocolate chips instead.*

barbecue snack mix

prep time: **10 minutes** ▪ start to finish: **30 minutes** ▪ **30 servings** (¼ cup each)

3 cups Rice Chex cereal

3 cups Corn Chex cereal

1½ cups pretzel twists

1½ cups bite-size cheese
   crackers

¾ cup honey-roasted
   peanuts

½ cup barbecue sauce

1 tablespoon vegetable oil

¾ teaspoon onion powder

¾ teaspoon garlic powder

1 In large microwavable bowl, mix cereals, pretzels, crackers and peanuts. In medium bowl, mix remaining ingredients until well blended. Pour over cereal mixture, stirring until evenly coated.

2 Microwave uncovered on High 10 minutes, stirring every 3 minutes. Spread on aluminum foil or paper towels until cooled. Store in airtight container.

1 SERVING: Calories 80; Total Fat 3g (Saturated Fat 0.5g; Trans Fat 0g); Cholesterol 0mg; Sodium 170mg; Total Carbohydrate 11g (Dietary Fiber 0g); Protein 2g **EXCHANGES:** ½ Starch, ½ Fat **CARBOHYDRATE CHOICES:** 1

substitution idea *Use any combination of Chex cereal that your kids like.*

sunny honey snack mix

prep time: **15 minutes** ▪ start to finish: **30 minutes** ▪ **40 servings** (¼ cup each)

8 cups Corn Chex cereal

2 cups Honey Nut Cheerios cereal

½ cup roasted sunflower nuts

¼ cup butter or margarine

¼ cup honey

1½ cups pastel-colored candy-coated chocolate candies

1 In large microwavable bowl, mix cereals and sunflower nuts.

2 In 2-cup microwavable measuring cup, microwave butter and honey uncovered on High 1 to 2 minutes, stirring every 30 seconds, until mixture comes to a full boil and butter is melted. Pour over cereal mixture, stirring until evenly coated. Microwave uncovered on High 2 to 4 minutes, stirring every minute, until mixture is well coated and looks glazed.

3 Spread on waxed paper or foil; cool about 15 minutes. Place in serving bowl; stir in chocolate candies. Store in airtight container.

1 SERVING: Calories 100; Total Fat 4g (Saturated Fat 2g; Trans Fat 0g); Cholesterol 0mg; Sodium 90mg; Total Carbohydrate 14g (Dietary Fiber 0g); Protein 1g EXCHANGES: ½ Starch, ½ Other Carbohydrate, ½ Fat CARBOHYDRATE CHOICES: 1

DOUGHBOY TIPS

Here's an easy recipe for kids to help with. They can measure ingredients. Then have them spray the inside of the measuring cup with cooking spray so the honey will slide right out after measuring.

oven directions   *Heat oven to 300°F. In ungreased large roasting pan, mix cereals and sunflower nuts. In 1-quart saucepan, heat butter and honey over medium heat until boiling, stirring frequently. Pour over cereal mixture, stirring until evenly coated. Bake uncovered 25 to 30 minutes, stirring after 15 minutes, until mixture looks glazed. Spread on waxed paper or foil; cool about 15 minutes. Place in serving bowl; stir in chocolate candies. Store in airtight container.*

cheesy crescent ghosts

prep time: **20 minutes** · start to finish: **30 minutes** · 16 appetizers

1 can (8 oz) refrigerated crescent dinner rolls

1 cup shredded mozzarella cheese or Colby-Monterey Jack cheese blend (4 oz)

Assorted sliced olives and chiles, as desired

1 Heat oven to 375°F. Spray large cookie sheet with cooking spray, or cover with cooking parchment paper.

2 On cutting board, unroll dough and separate into 8 triangles. From center of longest side to opposite point, cut each triangle in half, making 16 triangles. Shape each as needed to look like ghost shape. Arrange triangles on cookie sheet, folding narrow point under about ½ inch, to form head of ghost.

3 Bake about 7 minutes or until slightly puffed and just beginning to brown. Sprinkle each ghost with 1 tablespoon cheese; top with sliced olives to form mouth and eyes. Bake 2 to 3 minutes longer or until cheese is melted.

1 APPETIZER: Calories 45; Total Fat 2.5g (Saturated Fat 1g; Trans Fat 0g); Cholesterol 0mg; Sodium 90mg; Total Carbohydrate 4g (Dietary Fiber 0g); Protein 2g **EXCHANGES:** ½ Other Carbohydrate, ½ Fat **CARBOHYDRATE CHOICES:** 0

DOUGHBOY TIPS

Be creative and use what you have on hand to add mouths and eyes to the ghosts—nuts, dill pickles or cut-up tomato will all work.

pizza pinwheels

prep time: **15 minutes** ▪ start to finish: **30 minutes** ▪ **24 servings** (1 appetizer and 1 teaspoon sauce each)

1 can (8 oz) refrigerated crescent dinner rolls

2 tablespoons grated Parmesan cheese

⅓ cup finely chopped pepperoni (about 1½ oz)

2 tablespoons finely chopped green bell pepper

½ cup shredded Italian cheese blend (2 oz)

½ cup pizza sauce

1 Heat oven to 350°F. Spray cookie sheet with cooking spray. Unroll dough and separate into 4 rectangles; firmly press perforations to seal.

2 Sprinkle Parmesan cheese, pepperoni, bell pepper and Italian cheese blend over each rectangle.

3 Starting with one short side, roll up each rectangle; press edge to seal. With serrated knife, cut each roll into 6 slices; place cut sides down on cookie sheet.

4 Bake 13 to 17 minutes or until edges are golden brown. Meanwhile, heat pizza sauce. Immediately remove pinwheels from cookie sheet. Serve warm with warm pizza sauce for dipping.

1 SERVING: Calories 60; Total Fat 3.5g (Saturated Fat 1.5g; Trans Fat 0.5g); Cholesterol 0mg; Sodium 140mg; Total Carbohydrate 4g (Dietary Fiber 0g); Protein 2g EXCHANGES: ½ Starch, ½ Fat CARBOHYDRATE CHOICES: 0

DOUGHBOY TIPS

Have the kids take turns sprinkling on the toppings, and then show them how to roll up the dough.

substitution idea *These bite-size pinwheels can also be made with shredded mozzarella cheese instead of the Italian blend.*

from snacks to treats anytime

When the all-too-familiar phrase "Mom, I'm hungry!" is heard, you want to be ready with food that pleases. And because snacking can be an important part of a daily diet, healthy alternatives are definitely a plus. Here are some top picks for snacks that are good for kids and taste good too.

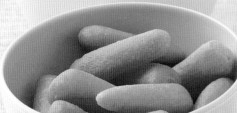

- Cucumber slices
- Baby carrots
- Grape or cherry tomatoes
- Broccoli florets
- Pitted olives
- Dried fruits
- Peanuts—plain or honey-roasted
- Sunflower seeds
- Roasted soynuts
- Pretzels

- Low-fat cheese slices or cubes
- Air-popped popcorn
- Small cans of light fruit
- Melon cubes
- Rice cakes
- Celery or whole grain crackers topped with peanut butter or

- low-fat cream cheese and raisins
- Open-faced sandwiches cut with cookie cutter and topped with apple butter
- Small containers of fat-free pudding
- Fat-free frozen yogurt or ice cream

crunchy mummies

prep time: **30 minutes** ▪ start to finish: **30 minutes** ▪ **20 servings**

1⅓ cups low-fat garden vegetable cream cheese spread, softened

20 pieces (3½ inches each) celery

3 slices (1 oz each) deli sliced cooked ham

10 sweetened dried cranberries

1 Place cream cheese in resealable food-storage plastic bag. Cut ½ inch off 1 corner. Pipe about 1 tablespoon into each celery piece.

2 Cut ham slices lengthwise into 16 pieces. Cut pieces crosswise into 1-inch pieces. Place about 12 ham pieces over cream cheese to look like "bandages" and use tip of knife to tuck in ends of ham along celery edge.

3 Cut cranberries into 40 pieces. Place pieces between "bandages" for eyes.

1 SERVING: Calories 40; Total Fat 2.5g (Saturated Fat 1.5g; Trans Fat 0g); Cholesterol 10mg; Sodium 130mg; Total Carbohydrate 2g (Dietary Fiber 0g); Protein 2g **EXCHANGES:** ½ Fat **CARBOHYDRATE CHOICES:** 0

 DOUGHBOY TIPS

These cute snacks are fun for kids to make and eat. Cut a thin slice from the bottom of the celery so it lays flat. Then if you want, serve the mummies on whole grain crackers.

super FAST | herbed cheese dip

prep time: **15 minutes** • start to finish: **15 minutes** • **14 servings** (2 tablespoons dip each)

1 package (8 oz) fat-free cream cheese

½ cup plain fat-free yogurt

2 teaspoons milk

¼ cup finely chopped fresh parsley

3 tablespoons finely chopped fresh chives

2 tablespoons finely chopped fresh basil leaves

⅛ teaspoon garlic salt

Raw vegetable dippers or crackers, as desired

1 In small bowl, beat cream cheese, yogurt and milk using electric mixer on low speed until blended.

2 Fold in parsley, chives, basil and garlic salt. Serve immediately with dippers, or cover and refrigerate until serving time.

1 SERVING: Calories 40; Total Fat 2.5g (Saturated Fat 1.5g; Trans Fat 0g); Cholesterol 10mg; Sodium 90mg; Total Carbohydrate 2g (Dietary Fiber 0g); Protein 2g EXCHANGES: ½ Fat CARBOHYDRATE CHOICES: 0

substitution idea *For adventurous snackers, a soft mild goat cheese (such as Montrachet) can be substituted for the cream cheese.*

super FAST | fresh tomato and chile salsa

prep time: **10 minutes** ▪ start to finish: **10 minutes** ▪ **12 servings** (¼ cup each)

4 medium tomatoes, chopped (3 cups)

1 serrano or jalapeño chile, seeded, finely chopped

1 tablespoon finely chopped onion

1 tablespoon chopped fresh cilantro

1 teaspoon fresh lime juice

½ teaspoon salt

Tortilla chips, as desired

1 In medium bowl, mix all ingredients except tortilla chips until blended.

2 Cover and refrigerate until serving time. Serve with tortilla chips.

1 SERVING: Calories 10; Total Fat 0g (Saturated Fat 0g; Trans Fat 0g); Cholesterol 0mg; Sodium 100mg; Total Carbohydrate 2g (Dietary Fiber 0g); Protein 0g EXCHANGES: Free CARBOHYDRATE CHOICES: 0

good eats for kids   *Nutritious tomatoes are the base for this yummy, slightly spicy dip. It's low in calories, rich in vitamin C and is fat-free. Try baked tortilla chips—they're lower in fat than the fried ones.*

super FAST | creamy low-calorie dill dip

prep time: **10 minutes** ▪ start to finish: **10 minutes** ▪ **16 servings** (1 tablespoon each)

1 (8-oz.) container nonfat sour cream

¼ cup reduced-fat mayonnaise

2 teaspoons dried dill weed

1 teaspoon instant minced onion

1 teaspoon dried parsley flakes

Raw vegetable dippers, as desired

1 In small bowl, combine all ingredients; blend well.

2 Serve immediately, or refrigerate several hours to blend flavors. Serve with assorted vegetable dippers.

1 SERVING: Calories 25; Total Fat 1g (Saturated Fat 0g, Trans Fat 0g); Cholesterol 0mg; Sodium 45mg; Total Carbohydrate 3g (Dietary Fiber 0g); Protein 0g **EXCHANGES:** Free **CARBOHYDRATE CHOICES:** 0

creamy applesauce dip

prep time: **10 minutes** ▪ start to finish: **10 minutes** ▪ **4 servings** (2 tablespoons dip and 4 animal crackers each)

DIP

½ cup applesauce

2 tablespoons vanilla low-fat yogurt

⅛ teaspoon ground cinnamon

DIPPERS (CHOOSE YOUR FAVORITE)

Animal crackers

Chocolate graham crackers

Rainbow-colored vanilla wafers

Sweetened miniature shredded wheat cereal

1 In small bowl, mix dip ingredients.

2 Dip your favorite dippers in the dip.

1 SERVING: Calories 70; Total Fat 1.5g (Saturated Fat 0g; Trans Fat 0g); Cholesterol 0mg; Sodium 50mg; Total Carbohydrate 12g (Dietary Fiber 0g); Protein 1g **EXCHANGES:** ½ Starch, ½ Other Carbohydrate **CARBOHYDRATE CHOICES:** 1

substitution idea *The dip can also be sprinkled with a little nutmeg. Some other great dippers are apple and pear slices, fresh strawberries and dried apricots.*

chilling jack-o'-lantern smoothies

prep time: **15 minutes** • start to finish: **15 minutes** • **4 servings** (¾ cup each)

1 tablespoon semisweet chocolate chips

4 plastic cups (8 to 9 oz each)

3 containers (6 oz each) orange crème or harvest peach low-fat yogurt

¼ cup frozen (thawed) orange juice concentrate

1 can (11 oz) mandarin orange segments, chilled, drained

1 banana, sliced

1 In small microwavable bowl, heat chocolate chips uncovered on High about 1 minute or until chips can be stirred smooth. With tip of knife, spread chocolate on inside of each plastic cup to look like eyes, nose and mouth of jack-o'-lantern. Refrigerate about 5 minutes or until chocolate is set.

2 Meanwhile, in blender, place remaining ingredients. Cover; blend until smooth. Pour into chocolate-painted cups. Serve immediately.

1 SERVING: Calories 230; Total Fat 2g (Saturated Fat 1.5g; Trans Fat 0g); Cholesterol 10mg; Sodium 65mg; Total Carbohydrate 47g (Dietary Fiber 2g); Protein 5g EXCHANGES: ½ Fruit, 2½ Other Carbohydrate, ½ Skim Milk CARBOHYDRATE CHOICES: 3

DOUGHBOY TIPS

With a little supervision, kids can explore their artistic side making the faces inside the cups. It works best to place the cup on its side when painting the face. Serve with a green straw to look like a pumpkin stem or garnish with a little mint leaf.

super FAST | chill-out parfaits

prep time: **10 minutes** • start to finish: **10 minutes** • 2 parfaits

1 container (6 oz) thick and
creamy fat-free yogurt
(any flavor)

1 cup Cheerios cereal

2 bananas or other fresh
fruit, sliced

1 In 2 parfait glasses or cups, alternate layers of yogurt, cereal and bananas.

2 Serve immediately.

1 PARFAIT: Calories 260; Total Fat 2.5g (Saturated Fat 0.5g; Trans Fat 0g); Cholesterol 0mg; Sodium 160mg; Total Carbohydrate 54g (Dietary Fiber 5g); Protein 7g **EXCHANGES:** 1 Starch, 2 Fruit, ½ Low-Fat Milk **CARBOHYDRATE CHOICES:** 3½

good eats for kids *Rich in potassium and a good source of vitamin C, bananas are an ideal dessert for kids and adults alike. Here, they're combined with a whole grain cereal and calcium-rich yogurt for a power-packed treat.*

easy cocoa brownies

prep time: **30 minutes** • start to finish: **30 minutes** • **16 bars**

⅔ cup all-purpose flour

¾ cup granulated sugar

¼ cup unsweetened baking cocoa

¼ teaspoon baking powder

⅛ teaspoon salt

⅓ cup margarine or butter, melted

2 teaspoons vanilla

1 egg, slightly beaten

1 teaspoon powdered sugar

1 Heat oven to 350°F. Spray 8-inch square pan with cooking spray.

2 In large bowl, mix flour, granulated sugar, cocoa, baking powder and salt. Add margarine, vanilla and egg; stir just until mixed. Spread evenly in pan.

3 Bake about 18 minutes or just until set. DO NOT OVERBAKE. Sprinkle with powdered sugar. Cut into 4 rows by 4 rows. If desired, cut each square in half to make triangles. Serve warm or cool.

1 BAR: Calories 100; Total Fat 4.5g (Saturated Fat 1g; Trans Fat 0.5g); Cholesterol 15mg; Sodium 60mg; Total Carbohydrate 14g (Dietary Fiber 0g); Protein 1g **EXCHANGES:** ½ Starch, ½ Other Carbohydrate, 1 Fat **CARBOHYDRATE CHOICES:** 1

DOUGHBOY TIPS

Wrap these up for a lunchbox addition or an after-school treat.

super FAST | # granola fruit kabobs

prep time: **10 minutes** ▪ start to finish: **10 minutes** ▪ **8 servings**

2 cups granola

2 medium apples, unpeeled,
    cut into chunks

2 small bananas, peeled,
    cut into chunks

1 cup fresh pineapple
    chunks

1 cup Yoplait® Original
    fruit-flavored yogurt

1 Place granola in shallow bowl. Insert toothpick into each piece of fruit.

2 To serve, dip fruit into yogurt, coating all sides. Roll in granola, coating completely.

1 SERVING: Calories 200; Total Fat 5g (Saturated Fat 2g, Trans Fat 0g); Cholesterol 0mg; Sodium 30mg; Total Carbohydrate 35g (Dietary Fiber 4g); Protein 4g **EXCHANGES:** 1 Starch, ½ Fruit, 1 Other Carbohydrate, 1 Fat **CARBOHYDRATE CHOICES:** 2

DOUGHBOY TIPS

To prevent cut fruits such as bananas and apples from browning, toss the pieces with a small amount of lemon or orange juice.

lemony fruit dip

prep time: **10 minutes** ▪ start to finish: **1 hour 40 minutes** ▪ **6 servings** (¼ cup dip and ½ apple each)

¼ cup pineapple cream cheese spread

1 container (8 oz) lemon low-fat yogurt

¼ cup dried fruit and raisin mixture

3 large unpeeled apples, sliced

1 In small bowl, beat cream cheese and yogurt using electric mixer on low speed until blended. Stir in fruit and raisin mixture. Cover and refrigerate 20 minutes.

2 Divide dip among 6 custard cups. Serve with apple slices as dunkers.

1 SERVING: Calories 150; Total Fat 3.5g (Saturated Fat 2g; Trans Fat 0g); Cholesterol 10mg; Sodium 55mg; Total Carbohydrate 28g (Dietary Fiber 3g); Protein 2g **EXCHANGES:** 1 Fruit, 1 Other Carbohydrate, ½ Fat **CARBOHYDRATE CHOICES:** 2

DOUGHBOY TIPS

Because no cooking is involved with this recipe, it's perfect for kids to stir together.

substitution idea *Can you think of some other foods to dip into this fruity dip? How about orange or pear slices? Try sticking grapes on a toothpick and dunking them into the dip.*

caramel yogurt and apples

prep time: **25 minutes** ▪ start to finish: **25 minutes** ▪ **8 servings**

TOPPING

4 oz ⅓-less-fat cream cheese (Neufchâtel), softened

2 tablespoons powdered sugar

¼ cup vanilla low-fat yogurt

CARAMEL YOGURT

1 tablespoon margarine or butter

½ cup packed brown sugar

1 tablespoon light corn syrup

¼ cup evaporated fat-free milk or half-and-half

½ cup vanilla low-fat yogurt

APPLES

4 medium apples, coarsely chopped

1 In small bowl, beat cream cheese using electric mixer on low speed about 30 seconds or until fluffy. Add powdered sugar; gradually add ¼ cup yogurt, beating until smooth. Refrigerate while preparing caramel yogurt.

2 In 1-quart saucepan, melt margarine. Stir in brown sugar and corn syrup. Heat to boiling over medium heat, stirring constantly. Stir in milk. Return to boiling; boil 1 minute. Remove from heat; cool 5 minutes, stirring occasionally. Beat in ½ cup yogurt with whisk until smooth.

3 Divide chopped apples evenly among 8 dessert dishes. Spoon warm caramel yogurt over apples; top with topping. If desired, sprinkle with nutmeg.

1 SERVING: Calories 200; Total Fat 5g (Saturated Fat 2.5g; Trans Fat 0g); Cholesterol 10mg; Sodium 90mg; Total Carbohydrate 35g (Dietary Fiber 2g); Protein 3g **EXCHANGES:** ½ Starch, ½ Fruit, 1½ Other Carbohydrate, 1 Fat **CARBOHYDRATE CHOICES:** 2

substitution idea   *Do your kids like pears? They can be substituted for the apples.*

super FAST | cherry and peach cream cakes

prep time: **20 minutes** ▪ start to finish: **20 minutes** ▪ 8 servings

2 cups fresh sweet cherries, pitted

1 medium peach, peeled, cut into 1-inch pieces

⅓ cup peach spreadable fruit, melted

¾ cup peach low-fat yogurt

¼ cup fat-free sour cream

8 individual sponge shortcake cups

3 tablespoons orange juice

1 In medium bowl, toss cherries, peach and spreadable fruit to coat. In small bowl, mix yogurt and sour cream.

2 Place shortcake cups on 8 dessert plates. Sprinkle each with about 1 teaspoon orange juice. Spread about 1 to 2 tablespoons yogurt mixture evenly in each cup. Spoon fruit over yogurt mixture. Serve immediately.

1 SERVING: Calories 170; Total Fat 1.5g (Saturated Fat 0g; Trans Fat 0g); Cholesterol 40mg; Sodium 40mg; Total Carbohydrate 37g (Dietary Fiber 1g); Protein 3g **EXCHANGES:** 1 Starch, 1 Fruit, ½ Other Carbohydrate **CARBOHYDRATE CHOICES:** 2½

substitution idea *If you don't have fresh cherries, frozen, slightly thawed, cherries can be used instead.*

super FAST | caramel tropical sundaes

prep time: **15 minutes** ▪ start to finish: **15 minutes** ▪ **6 servings**

½ cup fat-free caramel topping

½ teaspoon imitation rum extract

4 slices (½-inch-thick) cored fresh pineapple

2 small bananas

3 cups fat-free vanilla ice cream or frozen yogurt

1 In 10-inch skillet, mix topping and rum extract. Cook over medium heat 1 to 2 minutes, stirring occasionally, until topping is melted and mixture is smooth.

2 Cut each pineapple slice into 6 wedges. Peel bananas; cut diagonally into ½-inch-thick slices. Gently stir pineapple and bananas into topping mixture. Cook over medium heat about 2 minutes, stirring gently, until fruit is hot.

3 Into each dessert dish, spoon ½ cup ice cream. Top each with fruit mixture.

1 SERVING: Calories 230; Total Fat 0g (Saturated Fat 0g; Trans Fat 0g); Cholesterol 0mg; Sodium 160mg; Total Carbohydrate 53g (Dietary Fiber 2g); Protein 4g **EXCHANGES:** 1 Starch, 1 Fruit, 1½ Other Carbohydrate **CARBOHYDRATE CHOICES:** 3½

substitution idea *Butterscotch topping would be a nice alternative to the caramel. Look for fresh pineapple already cored and peeled in the refrigerated produce aisle. Canned pineapple slices will work just fine too.*

baked apples with granola

prep time: **10 minutes** • start to finish: **15 minutes** • 2 servings

1 large crisp apple (such as Braeburn, Gala or Fuji)

1 tablespoon raisins or sweetened dried cranberries

1 tablespoon packed brown sugar

2 teaspoons margarine or butter, softened

½ cup low-fat fruit granola

1 Cut apple in half lengthwise. With spoon, remove and discard core, making at least a 1-inch indentation in each apple half. Place each half in small microwavable bowl.

2 Fill each apple half evenly with raisins and brown sugar; dot with margarine. Cover each with microwavable plastic wrap, venting one corner.

3 Microwave each apple half on High 2 minutes 30 seconds to 3 minutes or until apple is tender. Top each with granola. If desired, serve with a little milk, cream or fruit-flavored yogurt.

1 SERVING: Calories 240; Total Fat 5g (Saturated Fat 1g; Trans Fat 0.5g); Cholesterol 0mg; Sodium 40mg; Total Carbohydrate 46g (Dietary Fiber 4g); Protein 2g **EXCHANGES:** ½ Starch, 1 Fruit, 1½ Other Carbohydrates, 1 Fat **CARBOHYDRATE CHOICES:** 3

DOUGHBOY TIPS

What an ideal dessert treat for kids to make themselves. You can teach them how to cover with plastic wrap for microwaving. Let them sprinkle on their own granola at the end.

good eats for kids   *Apples are a good source of vitamins A and C, and taste great, too.*

helpful nutrition and cooking information

nutrition guidelines

We provide nutrition information for each recipe that includes calories, fat, cholesterol, sodium, carbohydrate, fiber and protein. Individual food choices can be based on this information.

recommended intake for a daily diet of 2,000 calories as set by the food and drug administration

Total Fat	Less than 65g
Saturated Fat	Less than 20g
Cholesterol	Less than 300mg
Sodium	Less than 2,400mg
Total Carbohydrate	300g
Dietary Fiber	25g

criteria used for calculating nutrition information

- The first ingredient was used wherever a choice is given (such as ⅓ cup sour cream or plain yogurt).
- The first ingredient amount was used wherever a range is given (such as 3- to 3½-pound cut-up broiler-fryer chicken).
- The first serving number was used wherever a range is given (such as 4 to 6 servings).
- "If desired" ingredients and recipe variations were not included (such as "sprinkle with brown sugar, if desired").
- Only the amount of a marinade or frying oil that is estimated to be absorbed by the food during preparation or cooking was calculated.

ingredients used in recipe testing and nutrition calculations

- Ingredients used for testing represent those that the majority of consumers use in their homes: large eggs, 2% milk, 80%-lean ground beef, canned ready-to-use chicken broth and vegetable oil spread containing not less than 65% fat.
- Fat-free, low-fat or low-sodium products were not used, unless otherwise indicated.
- Solid vegetable shortening (not butter, margarine, nonstick cooking sprays or vegetable oil spread as they can cause sticking problems) was used to grease pans, unless otherwise indicated.

equipment used in recipe testing

We use equipment for testing that the majority of consumers use in their homes. If a specific piece of equipment (such as a wire whisk) is necessary for recipe success, it is listed in the recipe.

- Cookware and bakeware without nonstick coatings were used, unless otherwise indicated.
- No dark-colored, black or insulated bakeware was used.
- When a pan is specified in a recipe, a metal pan was used; a baking dish or pie plate means ovenproof glass was used.
- An electric hand mixer was used for mixing only when mixer speeds are specified in the recipe directions. When a mixer speed is not given, a spoon or fork was used.

cooking terms glossary

beat Mix ingredients vigorously with spoon, fork, whisk, hand beater or electric mixer until smooth and uniform.

boil Heat liquid until bubbles rise continuously and break on the surface and steam is given off. For rolling boil, the bubbles form rapidly.

chop Cut into coarse or fine irregular pieces with a knife, food chopper, blender or food processor.

cube Cut into squares ½ inch or larger.

dice Cut into squares smaller than ½ inch.

grate Cut into tiny particles using small rough holes of grater (citrus peel or chocolate).

grease Rub the inside surface of a pan with shortening, using pastry brush, piece of waxed paper or paper towel, to prevent food from sticking during baking (as for some casseroles).

julienne Cut into thin, matchlike strips, using knife or food processor (vegetables, fruits, meats).

mix Combine ingredients in any way that distributes them evenly.

sauté Cook foods in hot oil or margarine over medium-high heat with frequent tossing and turning motion.

shred Cut into long thin pieces by rubbing food across the holes of a shredder, as for cheese, or by using a knife to slice very thinly, as for cabbage.

simmer Cook in liquid just below the boiling point on top of the stove; usually after reducing heat from a boil. Bubbles will rise slowly and break just below the surface.

stir Mix ingredients until uniform consistency. Stir once in a while for stirring occasionally, often for stirring frequently and continuously for stirring constantly.

toss Tumble ingredients (such as green salad) lightly with a lifting motion, usually to coat evenly or mix with another food.

metric conversion guide

volume

U.S. UNITS	CANADIAN METRIC	AUSTRALIAN METRIC
¼ teaspoon	1 mL	1 ml
½ teaspoon	2 mL	2 ml
1 teaspoon	5 mL	5 ml
1 tablespoon	15 mL	20 ml
¼ cup	50 mL	60 ml
⅓ cup	75 mL	80 ml
½ cup	125 mL	125 ml
⅔ cup	150 mL	170 ml
¾ cup	175 mL	190 ml
1 cup	250 mL	250 ml
1 quart	1 liter	1 liter
1½ quarts	1.5 liters	1.5 liters
2 quarts	2 liters	2 liters
2½ quarts	2.5 liters	2.5 liters
3 quarts	3 liters	3 liters
4 quarts	4 liters	4 liters

weight

U.S. UNITS	CANADIAN METRIC	AUSTRALIAN METRIC
1 ounce	30 grams	30 grams
2 ounces	55 grams	60 grams
3 ounces	85 grams	90 grams
4 ounces (¼ pound)	115 grams	125 grams
8 ounces (½ pound)	225 grams	225 grams
16 ounces (1 pound)	455 grams	500 grams
1 pound	455 grams	0.5 kilogram

measurements

INCHES	CENTIMETERS
1	2.5
2	5.0
3	7.5
4	10.0
5	12.5
6	15.0
7	17.5
8	20.5
9	23.0
10	25.5
11	28.0
12	30.5
13	33.0

temperatures

FAHRENHEIT	CELSIUS
32°	0°
212°	100°
250°	120°
275°	140°
300°	150°
325°	160°
350°	180°
375°	190°
400°	200°
425°	220°
450°	230°
475°	240°
500°	260°

Note: The recipes in this cookbook have not been developed or tested using metric measures. When converting recipes to metric, some variations in quality may be noted.

index

Page numbers in *italics* indicate illustrations

Hungry for more?
See what else
Pillsbury has to offer.

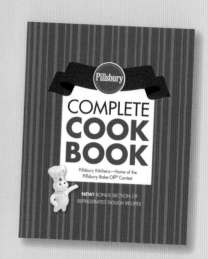

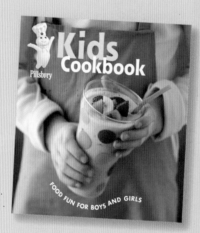

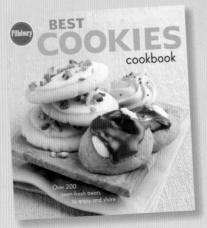